"My work with Mr. Shulman has been very enlightening! He guided me on a path of self-discovery and growth and offered the support that can only come from a person who has been there himself. Through the 10 sessions, I learned many new skills for living with this addiction, had the chance to try them out and then got to share my experiences in my next session. I felt that together we built a solid base for my recovery and I highly recommend Mr. Shulman's counseling." T.C., Chicago, Illinois

"I had a healing, cleansing experience by counseling with Mr. Shulman. He not only helped me understand why I had been stealing, but gave me the tools and the confidence to see the warning signs of future relapses. It was a life changing event. "" -David G., Port Huron, Michigan

"Mr. Shulman, you helped me begin my recovery journey and I thank you from the bottom of my heart. I have a new relationship with money now–I've even become a generous tipper! But most of all, I feel good about who I am. I feel at peace." -Diana W., Baton Rouge, Louisiana

"My willingness to change and Mr. Shulman's program have truly changed me. If I had known about this program earlier, I could have avoided so much pain, trouble and legal issues." Alondra C., New Orleans, Louisiana

"Mr. Shulman's compassion and non-judgmental ways made it easier for me to feel accepted with my addiction problem." -Amy G., Farmington Hills, Michigan

D1173268

BITING THE HAND THAT FEEDS

THE EMPLOYEE THEFT EPIDEMIC:
New Perspectives, New Solutions

**Terrence Daryl Shulman,
JD, MSW, CAC, CPC**

**Author of
SOMETHING FOR NOTHING:**
Shoplifting Addiction and Recovery

Copyright © 2005 by Terrence Daryl Shulman

All rights reserved. No part of this book shall be reproduced or transmitted in any form or by any means, electronic, mechanical, magnetic, photographic including photocopying, recording or by any information storage and retrieval system, without prior written permission of the publisher. No patent liability is assumed with respect to the use of the information contained herein. Although every precaution has been taken in the preparation of this book, the publisher and author assume no responsibility for errors or omissions. Neither is any liability assumed for damages resulting from the use of the information contained herein.

ISBN 0-7414-2723-0

Published by:

INFI∞ITY
PUBLISHING.COM

1094 New DeHaven Street, Suite 100
West Conshohocken, PA 19428-2713
Info@buybooksontheweb.com
www.buybooksontheweb.com
Toll-free (877) BUY BOOK
Local Phone (610) 941-9999
Fax (610) 941-9959

Printed in the United States of America

Published February 2009

<u>Dedication</u>

I dedicate this book to the millions of people around this world who have "bitten the hand that feeds" and to the families and friends who are affected as well. May this book serve as a lifeline to recovery. You are not alone. There is hope.

I also dedicate this book to the brave souls who have contributed their stories in this book, to those who have already sought help, and to those who have made a difference in the lives of others by seeing with curiosity, compassion and faith the pain and the hope in each other.

Table of Contents

Part Three
New Solutions

Part Four
Exercises for Recovering Theft Addicts

Part Five
Related Issues

Acknowledgments

As with my first book, there are so many people I wish to acknowledge. Please forgive me if I have forgotten any of you who have touched my life.

My beautiful & supportive wife, Tina,

My mother Madeline & my step-Dad Jim,

My brothers Jordy, Sam, and Marty,

My nephew Devan,

My father, Robert, rest in peace,

All of my relatives for their unconditional love and support,

Steve Campbell, mentor and friend, rest in peace,

My best buddies who have kept me strong and centered: Lee Anzicek, Tom Lietaert, John Stempien, Brett Koon, Dana L. Piper, Scott McWhinney, Marty Peters, Ben Goryca, Rob Koliner, Kevin Lauderdale, Dick Halloran, Josh Barclay, Tom Reedy, Chuck Pavey, Andrew Miller, Michael Fox, John Stempien, Paul Plamondon, & Joe Sulak.

Dana L. Piper for back cover photograph,

Cathy Dyer, of Mandalas Awakening, for book cover design,

My Goddess cheerleading squad: Julie Brydon, Laura Hansen-Koon, Andrea MacFarland, Sharon Harris, Bryn Fortune, Shanda Siegmund, Stacy Arsht-Fox, Mona Light, Robin Schwartz, Megan Powers, Cindy Chandler, Carol Klawson, Amy Goldstein, Daya Faith Walden, Cristina Pavey & Maureen McDonald,

i

Nancy Rabitoy of Better Direction Design,

Benji and Penelope, the love dogs,

My fellow recovering friends in C.A.S.A. (Detroit area),

My fellow recovering friends on C.A.S.A.'s e-mail group,

Secular Organization for Sobriety (S.O.S.),

Landmark Education Corporation, especially the Self-Expression & Leadership Course,

Stan Dale and the angels of the Human Awareness Institute,

The Detroit Area Men's Wisdom Council,

The Tuesday morning men's breakfast club,

The ManKind Project,

My friends at Personalized Nursing LIGHT House, Inc., (especially Marcia Andersen,)

Clean House Holistic Treatment Center,

Bert Whitehead, Carol Johnson, Pam Landy, & Jane Bertsch,

Dr. Eugene Ebner, PhD,

Dr. John Brownfain, PhD, rest in peace,

Elizabeth Corsale (Shoplifters Recovery Program),

Dr. Jon E. Grant,

Those who contributed their stories in this book, and

The folks at www.infinitypublishing.com.

About the Author

Terrence Daryl Shulman is a native Detroiter, an attorney, therapist, and consultant. He's been in recovery from addictive-compulsive stealing since 1990 and founded C.A.S.A. (Cleptomaniacs And Shoplifters Anonymous), a weekly support group, in 1992 in the Detroit area. C.A.S.A. is one of only a handful of such groups in the world.

He founded a theft addiction & recovery web site in 1995, now www.shopliftersanonymous.com, and the site www.employeetheftsolutions.com in 2004.

Mr. Shulman primarily counsels clients with theft addictions and disorders and their family members by phone and in person at his Detroit area office. He's worked extensively as a chemical dependency counselor and was a clinic Director.

Mr. Shulman consults within the retail industry and with companies to explore prevention, reduction and treatment strategies for shoplifting and employee theft.

He has been featured on various television programs, notably Oprah, Prime Time Live, 48 Hours, Fox Files, Inside Edition, Extra!, The Today Show, The Early Show, Ricki Lake, Queen Latifah, CNN News, Fox Cable News, The Discovery Channel and numerous local news programs.

He has been featured in over 100 magazines and newspaper articles including The New York Times, The Chicago Tribune, The Detroit Free Press, The Detroit News, The Metro Times, Lifetime, Health, Redbook, Cosmopolitan, Good Housekeeping TV Guide, Hour Magazine, O Magazine, Psychology Today, and Playboy.

He organized the First International Conference on Theft Addictions and Disorders in Detroit in 2005.

This is Mr. Shulman's second book.

He lives in Southfield, Michigan with his wife Tina.

Preface

My first book "Something for Nothing: Shoplifting Addiction and Recovery" (Infinity Publishing, 2004) took seven years–on and off–to write and publish. As with shoplifting, this book is about a similar epidemic–employee theft: both are far more than just moral, financial, or legal issues. Both books are intended as personal and professional offerings. As a therapist, attorney and consultant–and as one who intermittently shoplifted and stole from work from 1982-1990–I hope I have something unique and valuable to add to a new conversation on employee theft.

In September 2004, I appeared on The Oprah Winfrey Show to discuss my book and the topic of shoplifting addiction. Since then, my private counseling practice specializing in treating theft addictions and disorders has blossomed. Currently, I am awaiting an interview with ABC's Prime Time Live on the topic of shoplifting addiction, to be aired later this summer. And, finally, I am co-organizing and co-presenting at The First International Conference on Theft Addictions and Disorders in Detroit in the early fall.

I knew my second book would be on employee theft. I figured: one controversial topic at a time.

My first book emphasized shoplifting for several other reasons. First, roughly 75% of my own theft behavior took that form, compared to about 25% employee theft. Second, I'd met more people–personally and professionally–with shoplifting problems. Third, there was more interest: I'd had many more interviews in print, on radio and on TV about shoplifting than on employee theft. Finally, I didn't view employee theft as seriously. My consequences from shoplifting–two arrests, nearly having my law license withheld, among others–seemed more severe than losing a few jobs due to employee theft. Indeed, in re-reading my own story, I was shocked to realize during my entire course of therapy and conversations with family and friends, I completely neglected to share about my employee theft behaviors. As I did more research, I found the statistics on employee theft staggering. I now see it very seriously.

I've also had more time to look back on my work as an addictions therapist at a non-profit clinic from 1997-2004– with a stint as its Director from 1998-2000. I had the opportunity to live in the workplace culture over time. From time to time, I experienced a resurfacing of temptations to steal from work and, certainly, engaged in a few of the "lesser forms" of workplace theft. I'm sure, like many, I felt "they owe me."

As Director, I got to see my staff and the management from a middle-ground view. I got a closer glimpse of the politics of the workplace and how the bottom line is affected on every front. The pressures for everyone–including me–were enormous. By the time I resigned as Director in 2000, I realized I'd have to be self-employed one day–not only to reduce my temptation to steal again but to chart a path toward my higher potential–both financially and emotionally.

I will not be re-telling my life story here. If you are interested, you can read that in my first book. But a lot has happened in the two years since. Increasingly, I've worked with more people seeking help for chronic employee theft behaviors. As shoplifting recently has gained some relative acceptance as a potentially addictive and treatable behavior, people who steal from work have begun to seek help, too.

As in my own case, many people I've worked with have both shoplifted and committed employee theft–concurrently or at different stages. I'd estimate 50% of my clients have engaged in both forms of theft–to varying degrees; roughly 25% only shoplifted; roughly 15% only stole from work; and about 10% have done either credit card fraud or stolen from family, friends, or other individuals.

Interestingly, my clients often see either shoplifting as worse than employee theft or vice-versa. They've said: "I stole from a store–I had no business doing that. I could have gotten arrested and sent to jail. Everybody steals a little from work–you couldn't possibly fire everyone. Even the bosses do it." But I've also heard: "I feel so much lower than people who shoplift. They don't know the people they steal from. I know my boss, I know my co-workers. I have to walk into work each day feeling like I'm living a lie."

Does the kind of theft make a difference? What's worse: $5,000 worth of CD's shoplifted from stores or $5,000 worth of stamps and office supplies from work? Is stealing money worse than stealing items? It's all problematic for everyone! I hope to drive this point home.

Over the last two years I've also explored work as an independent loss prevention and corporate consultant. I thought if Frank Abagnale of "Catch Me If You Can" can turn his life around from a master fraud to a master consultant, so can I. In my research and in my discussions with those in various relevant fields, I've found most people don't care why people steal from work. They view any attempt to understand or explain theft as excuses. I have known countless people who didn't fully recognize they had a problem as well as those who knew they did and wanted to stop but didn't know how or where to go for help. I have a shared interest in seeing a reduction in theft; however, I have some different ideas about how to get there.

Employee theft is a hot potato right now. If the actress Winona Ryder dominated the headlines in 2002 during her shoplifting trial, we've had more than a decade of headlines on white collar crime and employee theft–from Enron to Martha Stewart. Most people are sick of excuses.

But it's not just the big stories that ought to concern us. Everyday, employee theft takes a bite out of us all.

Consider statistics from the American Society of Employers:

*Businesses lose 20% of every dollar to employee theft.

*20% of employees are aware of fraud at their companies (including theft of office items, false claims of hours worked, and inflated expense accounts).

*The average time it takes for an employer to catch a fraud scheme is 18 months.

*55% of perpetrators are managers.

*44% of workers say their companies could do more to reduce fraud.

*The U.S. Retail Industry loses $53.6 Billion a year due to employee theft.

*60% of companies have staff trained to deal with fraud and ethics issues (up from 30% in 2000).

Consider statistics from Jack Hayes International, Inc. 2007 Survey:

*In 2007, one in every 28.2 employees in U.S. was apprehended for theft from their employer.

*In 2007, 82,648 employees were apprehended from 24 large U.S. retail chains, up 17.57% from 2006.

The U.S. Chamber of Commerce estimates that 75% of all employees steal at least once, and that half of these steal again and again. The Chamber also reports that one of every three business failures are the direct result of employee theft.

In employee surveys conducted by academics, 43% of workers admitted stealing from their companies.

The FBI reports that employee theft is the fastest growing crime in the United States.

We need not worry solely about an enemy abroad taking a toll on our economy. We have met the enemy: it is us! It's either the worst time or the best time to start talking about this topic in a new way. I'm hoping it's the right time.

Terry Shulman,
Southfield, Michigan
July 2005

Introduction

Consider these excerpts from the following article in The Detroit Free Press, June 24, 2005:

Janis Fernworn, 45, was the treasurer for her church. Over several years, she embezzled at least $700,000. She appeared to have no history of alcohol, drug, or gambling addictions. She is married, has five children–two of them adopted–and lives in a wealthy suburb.

"I am horrified at what I did to my church. I pray they will someday forgive me for these repugnant crimes." Mrs. Fernworn and her husband had been members of the church for 23 years and her husband had served on the church's board.

According to prosecutors, Fernworn wrote checks to herself from church funds. She tried to hide this in various ways but was eventually discovered.

Fernworn said her embezzlement began when she and her husband were three months behind in paying their home mortgage. "I still remember the first time I wrote a check to myself that wasn't legitimate," she said. "My hands shook so badly, I was almost unable to manage the writing. I felt that I had exhausted all other possibilities. I don't know when it was that the embezzlement switched from easing the true need to needing the ease, but it didn't take long before the hole was so big that I couldn't face making it better."

Fernworn swore that she kept the embezzlement from her husband, who has not been charged.

The judge found it hard to believe he didn't know. "How could anyone live under the same roof and have $700,000 of tax-free income and not have clue Number 1 that something strange was going on?"

The church pastor asked the judge to send her to prison not out of revenge but saying "it is a price she must pay."

Because she had no prior offenses, her sentencing guidelines called for no more than 9 months in jail. The judge exceeded that and sent her to prison for 5-10 years.

This kind of story happens every day across the nation...

If you felt the judge in this case didn't give Janis Fernworn enough prison time, this book may not be for you. If you felt: what's the big deal?–this book also may not be for you. Or, maybe, after reading this book, you will see things differently. If you are able or are willing to see the tragedy for everyone–for Mrs. Fernworn, her husband, her kids, the church members, and the community–and new ways of reducing theft, then this book is talking to you.

We've all heard similar stories of the person fired from his or her job for embezzling some "ungodly" amount of money or stealing goods and product. Sure, there are greedy folks, plain thieves, and career criminals in our work force. But mostly, employee theft tends to happen a little at a time. Someone's vulnerable–there's a financial or emotional stressor, a conflict at work–and a line is crossed. Next thing you know, a star employee is hauled away in handcuffs. We scratch our heads, wondering: "What were they thinking? They didn't actually think they could get away with that?" The answer usually is: "They weren't thinking. They got hooked." *Employee theft can become addictive!*

There are plenty of books out there which quote facts, statistics, cursory reasons why people steal from work, and what can be done to reduce or prevent it. They may certainly be of value if that is primarily what the reader is looking for.

Most are written by "experts" in the security and loss prevention fields–the typical readers are store and business owners and fellow security and loss prevention folks.

This book is not about excusing employee theft. *But it is a different kind of book.* My intention is to make the topic relevant, provocative, and urgent for everyone!

Now, answer this question:

Have you ever committed employee theft? Yes or No?

How would you define employee theft? Is it only the blatant embezzlement and/or stealing of valuable assets from work? Is it a matter of degrees?

Be honest, have you ever done any of the following without the expressed permission from an employer?

*Fudged your time card?

*Padded an expense account or report?

*Made personal phone calls on company time?

*Used company postage?

*Used office supplies for personal use?

*Took office items home?

*Borrowed funds for personal use?

*Made personal copies on the copier?

*Failed to report accounting/payment errors in your favor?

*Used the company car for personal business?

*Ran errands on company time?

Chances are, you are in the 75% or more of all employees who have stolen from work.

What did one loss prevention worker say to another loss prevention worker?

The following was taken from an actual e-mail conversation:

One says: "No disrespect, but when we interview people who have been caught stealing–isn't finding out why they did it one of the most important reasons? By learning how people think, can't that help us both with better loss prevention strategies as well as recognizing if jail or some kind of education, diversion, or treatment programs might help reduce theft?"

The other says: "Internal theft or external theft, I don't care "WHY!" We have taken a lot of time and effort to enact loss prevention policies and procedures. When those are intentionally circumvented and it's time for me to sit people down and interview them about their actions–why they stole is my least concern if it is a concern at all. I'm concerned with facts! I am not a cold-hearted automaton. I treat everybody with the utmost respect! But I don't care why you stole. I'm just damn glad I caught you! ("you" meaning "bad guy.") You provide me with job security and because you and people like you exist, I get to come back to work tomorrow. My priority is to learn more about prevention and detection techniques. I don't wish to waste my time getting all squishy about the plights of individuals. Anyone who steals is a criminal."

It's not "either/or"– it's "both/and."

Imagine facing a problem like cancer or war. Indeed, we do so almost every day. We certainly need to take action to confront and arrest the effects of a disease or conflict in progress, hopefully learning more advanced and effective techniques each day. Likewise, it seems to me we must also adopt a comprehensive approach if we hope to make a lasting difference. If we know more about why cancers take root and why wars begin, wouldn't that be valuable, too? We constantly research genetics and lifestyle choices to learn more about how diseases occur. We study war history to prevent history from repeating itself. Indeed, we educate about "aftercare" treatment with diseases to best insure they don't return; we speak much of what is needed–and, hopefully, take measured steps–to "keep the peace" long after the fighting has stopped.

Even in our "war on drugs"–to the degree it has been effective–we've taken at least a two-prong approach: tough enforcement and penalties along with more education and treatment. Some argue there's not enough energy to do both. Others say doing both sends mixed messages. And others are thinking "outside the box" about causes and solutions.

Imagine you are someone who steals from work. You come to work each day with butterflies in your stomach, on edge, looking over your shoulder, wondering if today may be the day you are discovered. Every time your name is called, or the boss asks you a question, your gut tightens. Is this any way to live? Part of you wants to come clean, spill the beans, and stop the madness–but there's something that seems to stop you. Was this the life you chose?

Imagine you are a store or business owner and you are so busy you don't have the time to check every thing out. You do your best–in your mind–to treat your employees well and you think you can trust the people you employ but you can't. It's heart-breaking.

Imagine you are a loss prevention worker and going to work each day is like coming into a war zone. You can't let your guard down–you've been surprised and shocked before. You have become jaded and cynical. You long for the day when work is easier but you crave the challenge, too: you get a high from catching people who steal.

When shall we experience our "crash" moment–where each of our lives intersects and we feel each others' struggles in a new way?

Most companies just fire any employee who steals. I'm not saying acts of theft should go unpunished. But if nearly two thirds of employees are stealing on some level, we can't just fire everyone. Companies risk losing people who may not be easily replaced. They also risk losing a human touch. Also, an employee fired for theft will likely go to another company and steal due to the increasing reluctance of all companies to offer any prior work references, good or bad. We're living in an age where we "pass the buck"–"it's not my problem anymore." But we all live in the same world.

My hope is with more open open-minded conversation and more resources available, we shall see a transformation in the awareness of how we view theft behaviors. Then, and only then, will we be able to develop true loss prevention strategies and attain a more honest society and world.

This book is divided into five parts:

Part One highlights stories of those on various sides of the employee theft epidemic: the people who steal, the loss prevention people who try to stop them, and the store/business owners: a human face on theft.

Part Two provides a guide to various reasons why people steal from work, important data, statistics, and the challenges and issues that arise: new perspectives.

Part Three provides some progressive strategies to reducing and treating employee theft: new solutions.

Part Four includes exercises to help people stop stealing and move toward greater peace and wholeness: recovery.

Part Five focuses on related topics which did not fit as well in the other parts.

Part One

A Human Face on Theft

Aaron's Story

Aaron, 25, is a tall, sharp young man who has attended C.A.S.A. for over a year. He is now an assistant manager with a major retail superstore. He also does loss prevention.

My Mom raised me since age 8 when my father passed away from lung cancer. He got sick when I was about six and there was a long time where I didn't know what was going to happen with him. I was too young to understand. He went through all the surgeries, chemotherapy. But by the time he passed away in 1988 I realized he wasn't coming back.

I hated that my Dad was taken away from me. My brother was closer with my Mom; he still had his main influence in his life. I didn't. He was gone. My Mom did her best to fill my void with friends, family, people from the church, and a baseball player who worked with delinquents. That helped a little. But I didn't do well in school after my Dad's death. My Mom wouldn't let me get a job until my grades got better.

I began stealing around the age of 12 by shoplifting with some friends. One of them introduced me to it and then I told another one. We started off with small things like CD's, candy. We just wanted it and didn't want to pay. The first time I was caught shoplifting was a short time after I started. I got a slap on the wrist: thirty hours of community service and I had to report to a counselor. My record was expunged as if it never happened. Then I started to shoplift again but found ways to avoid getting caught. It just kept escalating all the way until I graduated high school.

1

As I got older, it got more serious and I started shoplifting on my own. I stole for myself as well as sold things I stole. Somebody would mention something they wanted and I knew I could get away with it, get it for them, and make some money off it. I stole just about anything–clothing, socks, shoes, whole outfits. Clothing was the big thing for me. My Mom wouldn't buy the things I wanted. So I just took them myself. I didn't have a job or much income. I was too young to work and my Mom didn't want me to anyway.

I became engaged to a woman, joined the military, and moved from Michigan to Virginia. I stopped stealing for a while because I had a new focus in my life and wanted to live life the way the military wanted me to live it. I belonged to the government and wanted to serve my country the right way. I had structure, free room and board, and put money aside. I didn't want to screw up something so good.

One day I found out my fiancée had cheated on me. She wanted to break off our engagement and go with this new guy. *I was crushed.* That's when things started going down hill with the military. I started not showing up on time, not doing things right. A lot of bad things started to happen because I was so upset. I became more focused on how to fix my life and get back in the game. I started to fall back in the habit of doing the old stuff again–shoplifting.

I began moonlighting at a fast food restaurant and a department store to take my mind off things when I had down time from the military. I used to call the department store the "Super Center" because they had everything there. Within a couple of months, I found myself stealing from the auto department. Once I crossed a line with employee theft, I noticed the employees weren't really being watched. I stole alone but knew other employees were doing the same thing. They had electronic gates so I took things right out the exit of the garden center which was wide open.

I got a rush or a high but also a feeling of nervousness–like is somebody going to catch me? But the rush or high came more after I felt sure I'd gotten away with it. Even in the parking lot it wasn't the time. But when I got home, the rush or the high of succeeding was enormous.

In the military I'd been trained in "Special Ops"–exercises where you don't want to be seen or known. Stealing became a test of whether or not my training was good enough.

I've never taken cash from stores I've worked at or taken people's money or wallets. I've never had a drug or gambling problem. I just seemed to take things.

I left the job at the Super Center after six months. I was working too many hours and wanted more time to party. I didn't miss my easy access to stealing as I still stole as a customer because I was still known there. When a stranger walks through the door–that's one thing; but when you're known and people like you, they'd never suspect you. I don't think any employees ever got caught.

Soon after leaving that job, I started dating a new girl. Her father was also in the military and things were going pretty well. Life seemed back on track. I forgot about stealing for a while. But then she and I broke up. I didn't realize it then but I became vulnerable again.

My roommate in the military used to leave our room late at night a lot–at 1 or 2 in the morning. I thought it was suspicious. Finally, I asked him about it and he told me he was breaking into people's homes and taking things. He'd either pawn or sell things. At first that seemed over the line for me. But I started asking him questions and guess I was convinced he had a full-proof way of getting away with it.

We broke into three houses together and took a bunch of belongings. There were no cars in the driveway or garage of the next house but when we got upstairs we heard snoring. I

3

thought "uh-oh, what would happen if they woke up–would I run or fight back? I told myself this was the last job I'd do.

But a few days later, we went back to the same house–my friend convinced me the owners were on vacation. Apparently, there were neighbors watching the house who got my license plate number. Eventually, we were both caught. It's funny, I was stealing but I've never been a liar. I was scared and they preyed on my "integrity" about telling the truth. They pieced two-and-two together and we got charged with the other three break-ins as well. My total sentence was 18 years; all but one of them was suspended, so I served about a year.

When I got out of jail, I was 21. I told myself "I'm never stealing again." I moved back to Michigan to start a whole new life. I just worked a lot–my idea was to make as much money as I could to move out of my Mom's home. I met a girl and we lived together for almost three years. Then we broke up and she moved to Mexico. I honestly believed I was in love with this girl. She was the one I wanted to marry.

Then, right afterwards, I stole from work–a sporting goods store. I stole almost $800 worth of hockey equipment. There were no cameras and I just walked out the back door with it. I had no idea I'd been watched by an employee–employees got rewarded for turning others in. Before the end of the shift, the cops showed up and–because I'm no liar–I told them where the stuff was: in the trunk of my car. I could have tried to beat the case or fought jail time but I was always taught by my mother–as well as by the military– to tell the truth. I don't know why the same thing didn't sink in about stealing. I got sentenced to a year in jail but was it was suspended and I got probation, 15 days of community service, and I had to take some education class.

Eventually, I got back with my ex-girlfriend; we were together only 10 days. I've been stealing-free for nearly a year and a half at this point. I've been determined not to let something like a break-up trigger me to steal. I'm positive my attendance at C.A.S.A. meetings over the last year and a half has taught me about my triggers–like losses–that can set me off again. I don't want to make the same mistake again.

Besides the legal consequences, my stealing has taken a real toll on my family. I feel responsible for my younger brother following in my footsteps. My stealing has put a strain on my mother. I've lost a couple of jobs and I've had problems getting jobs. One job let me go when I applied for a promotion and they did a background check. Recently, I was an assistant manager at another job where they also hadn't done a background check. Things were going really well. Then, by chance, they found out about my arrest at the sporting goods store by reading it in the local newspaper. I was fired though I'd never stolen from that company, never even thought about it. It didn't matter. They didn't trust me.

I was out of work for three months–I felt drained emotionally and spiritually. I didn't think anyone would hire me. I was desperate and filled out applications everywhere. It's interesting but I didn't shoplift during the three months I was off work. I'm sure I thought about it but I think the C.A.S.A. meetings helped me. I kept telling myself it wasn't worth it and I didn't want to go back to where I was before. I wasn't willing to allow myself to let that happen again.

Finally, I got a job about nine months ago at a national chain store. When the phone call came for this job, I was ready. They must not have done a background check–which is hard to believe. If they do one after the fact, I don't know what they'll do. It's possible they've already done it and decided to keep me on because I'm a good employee. I don't know. I do find it odd–I'm on the assistant manager track and some of my job involves loss prevention work. It actually keeps me in check. If I were to steal, I realize I wouldn't just be hurting them, I'd be hurting myself.

Loss prevention is important to our company as it's the

easiest way to affect profit. They put the employees through a lot of training about theft prevention. Yet, on the other hand, it seems like it's put on the back burner–like "yes, it's important, but we have a holiday coming up." We also have electronic gates that don't really work well. They get set off by a cell phone but not by the products with the sensors. Even since we got the U-Scan machines in, we've had some problems with customers not running things through. And our garden center is still a problem: people can just walk right out. Even in the winter–if you can get over the fence, you're out of there. We haven't fixed any of these problems so loss prevention doesn't always seem like a top priority.

Our store seems to go through cycles–we used to be more concerned about employee theft than shoplifting. But since they cleaned house not long ago, they're more concerned about shoplifting now. I think it should be more even but I do think we have a pretty good staff–we've hired people who seem more interested in working than standing around. I don't think our employees have enough time to think much about stealing. I don't even think any employee has been fired since I've been hired. Before I arrived, I heard some employees allowed friends or family to come in and they would undercharge or under-ring up.

Our store has a zero tolerance policy with shoplifting and employee theft. I got questioned about something the other day. I rang up a customer on an item and she told me it was on sale and brought me the sign. I marked it down and it was more than 50% off and it automatically triggered something with loss prevention. Within half an hour, they were on top of it and I had to explain to them what happened.

We have greeters at the entrances and exits and I think that helps deter theft. We also have a 10-foot rule where if an employee comes within 10-feet of a customer we have to ask if the customer needs any help. We want to treat our customers well. We try not to look at shoplifters as plain thieves. We see people addicted to drugs, or people who don't have much money. We also see shoplifters who are dressed in nice suits–we know some people have problems. We try to treat people professionally; sometimes we'll give a kid a lecture. I don't think our store knows about C.A.S.A. or treatment options. Frankly, I'm not sure they'd care.

Our loss prevention people try to do their best. Our company sends them around the country to seminars. They're on quota system, though. They get points for apprehensions and if they don't keep up, they'll be transferred to another department. There are a lot of rules and guidelines we have to follow so there are no false accusations or arrests. We have to be so careful. It's got to be a real clean catch. We have a lot of cameras but they're not always working or people aren't always manning them.

Our employees generally seem happy with their work but there's some grumbling, especially among newer employees who are paid a lot less than the "old timers." As a person who used to steal, I'm in an interesting position. I can identify with some of the people who steal but I also feel a loyalty to the store and, I admit, it's frustrating when I know someone has stolen something and they get away with it because I couldn't prove it. But when we wrongfully accuse someone, it's serious. It causes embarrassment to the customer and company. The customer's business is valued.

I actually feel justified catching shoplifters. I don't feel bad about it even if it's only a couple of bucks. I'd rather make sure the product is returned and let them know they don't have the right to do that. I'd rather let the police deal with it most of the time. There's been a few times where I haven't turned somebody in–like when I see someone eating our food in the store, I confront it but don't turn them in.

I'm just glad I'm not on the other side anymore–I'm not stealing. I have peace of mind for the first time in my life and a true sense of pride in myself and confidence about my future.

Notes & Reflections:

Madelon's Story

Madelon is 33, boisterous and out-spoken. She works as a babysitter and as a massage therapist. She has been in Alanon meetings and therapy for many years but only recently began her recovery from theft behaviors. She was fired from a job two years ago for embezzling $15,000.

I started stealing when I was 7 years old. I come from a wealthy family and neighborhood. I've been in Alanon for over 7 years and in recovery from stealing for nearly 3 years. I've been "theft-free" for a year and a half. My early stealing was mostly shoplifting and employee theft. I also did a credit card theft once. Then I "graduated" to stealing money from people's purses and embezzled money from a friend I worked for. I was fired two years ago.

There have been so many negative consequences in my life due to stealing. I've been arrested, I've lost friendships, and I lost a really good job as an office manager. But, most importantly, I lost the ability to grow as a good person, a mature person, and to get to another level of liking myself. I lost the ability to take care of myself–I neglected that for a very long time. My whole life has been about my addiction and my denial of my addiction. *I lived two different lives.*

It's amazing to look back on my life now. I can't believe I stole as much and as often as I did. I could blame my stealing on so many things but, really, I'm just trying to understand how and why I started. I know when I was a small child I saw my mother steal. She shoplifted and stole from people she worked for. She was a cleaner and stole toilet paper, food, laundry detergent, money–whatever she could get her hands on. She didn't need to steal–we had money.

My mother was brought up in a very unloving family. She had a "hole in her heart"–she didn't feel loved. I think she stole to try to fill that hole. Her parents didn't want her–she was an accident. Her mother survived the Holocaust and was always afraid of never having enough food. I found out my Mom had to steal food from people's gardens growing up. She was used to stealing from a very early age–just to survive. I think an equal part of it was also about her anger over life's injustices.

I learned the same thing. I've always felt something was taken away from me unjustly and I needed to fill up that hole. Drugs and alcohol never did it for me–I guess I was always afraid of them. Stealing has always been my really good friend, something I could fall back on. It felt good to have everything I wanted–which is what my disease told me–but that was a lie. It doesn't feel good to take things that don't belong to you. You can't really feel good about yourself. I felt a false good, a facade of the truth.

My mother never directly encouraged me steal but she did it in front of me. I remember she was always being investigated for stealing. But they could never really prove it. Things always appeared in our house that didn't make sense.

My father knew about it but didn't do anything. I don't think he stole but some people thought he was dishonest in business. He was–and is–an alcoholic.

One time when we were at the grocery store, a manager from the store followed us out and wrote my Mom's license plate number down. Another time, at K-Mart, my mother tried to hide something in my brother's stroller. She was caught and questioned but she blamed it on my father, saying "he made me do it." These days, she would have been taken to jail.

My earliest memory of stealing was when I was 7 years old. There was this girl in my neighborhood whose Mom owned a pet store. She had a ridiculous amount of animals–several cats and dogs, even a goat. My dog had just died. I stole one of her dogs, put it in the basket on my bicycle, and rode home. They knew I'd taken the dog and called my mother. She said, "Yes, the dog is here." I fell in love with her dog and felt it wasn't fair this girl had all those dogs and I didn't have any. I guess I tried to rectify the situation by stealing. It didn't work out that way. Everyone in my school found out. I was humiliated. My mother and father beat me. They labeled me a thief. It was considered the worst thing I could do.

But this didn't stop me from stealing again. I wished it hadn't become public news. I wished they'd forgiven me because I was just a kid. If I had a kid now who did that, I would have tried to understand and deal with it more compassionately. I was very angry at my Mom because I felt she was a hypocrite: she taught me how to steal and still stole herself–but I was punished. "Do as I say, not as I do."

When my parents divorced–I was young–it got even worse. My younger brother knew about all the stealing and he started doing it, too. Of course, nobody talked about it–it was swept under the rug. My Dad remarried and, somehow, he always picked wives who stole–my Mom stole, his second wife stole, and his third wife stole from nursing homes.

My mother, my brother, and I lived together in a small apartment after the divorce. My Mom and I shared a bedroom. It was awful. She was always in and out of my stuff–I never had my own stuff, not even my own dresser. I think I stole to have some of my own stuff. I'd go to the local drug store a lot and steal perfume and high-end items from behind the counter. I was good at it and did it a lot. I'd steal these things and hide them but she'd always find them. She knew I couldn't afford them. On many occasions, she'd humiliate me by taking me back to the store and make me return things. But she was stealing from the same store. I really resented her for that.

My Mom and I never went shopping together. We never went to mother-daughter lunches. She disliked me and I disliked her. I wanted a mother but she was never there for me. She went to the grocery store every day to steal. She stole clothes, too. I basically had to support myself. Even though she stole groceries, somehow there'd never be any food in the house. It took me a long time to realize she was actually depriving me of food. I stole money from her so I could buy food to bring back or to eat at a restaurant.

I feel this led to my dysfunctional relationship with food. I'm an overeater, a closet eater. My mother was also a closet eater though she wasn't as overweight as I am. It's similar to my stealing: both my behaviors were largely secretive. I also denied or minimized how much I stole or ate. Both behaviors temporarily helped me escape my pain. When I'm angry or depressed, I tend to eat and steal more, too. Both have led to negative consequences. I gained so much weight I became diabetic. There are a lot of correlations.

My mother was so abusive and I was so afraid of her that–at 15–I ran away from home. I came back not long afterwards when one of my friends suggested: "Why don't you just hit your Mom back?" So I did. She had hit me and I hit her back hard. That was the only time I ever confronted her. I said to her: "I know you steal. I know you're a thief."

I've come to believe my mother hated herself and she saw herself in me when I stole and that's why she reacted the way she did. She knew she couldn't stop and I think she knew in her heart she was the one who taught me how to steal. I don't think as a younger person I had much real choice in my actions. She never sought help and she always blamed everything that went wrong on me. I felt totally unloved and neglected and I stole to numb my pain.

As I began to shoplift more with friends my age, it felt very fun and very exciting. After the divorce, my Mom and Dad had stopped buying me things. I could just steal anything I wanted. I remember one time breaking into a jewelry store with a friend–her family owned the store. We stole a lot of jewelry. I remember another time I broke into the locker of a friend and took some money. I always denied it but she never forgave me. I even stole from a girl's purse during my high school graduation ceremony. Another friend saw me do this and was horrified and never wanted to talk to me again.

In 1992 I did my only credit card fraud. I was at a salon and a woman got up for a few minutes and left her purse; I reached inside it and grabbed a credit card. After leaving the store, I went right down the road and bought a pair of shoes and gas for my car. Then I got rid of the card. The woman must have noticed her card was missing when she went to pay at the salon; she called to cancel it but I'd already used it.

I must have wanted to get caught–the following week I went back to the salon. They called the woman from the shoe store; she came in to positively identify me. The police were called; I was fingerprinted and my mug shot taken.

I retained a lawyer and, because I was young and living at home, I got a break: two years probation which got reduced to 6 months. *But it was the most horrible, excruciating time in my life.* I had no support system, no one to turn to, and I had to borrow money and lie about why I was borrowing it. It was so humiliating. I swore I'd never do that again. I knew I needed to talk to a therapist but I didn't have the money.

I stopped stealing for two years but got a job at two retail stores and started stealing from work. I worked at a gift store where we all hated the manager. She stole, too, and let us take a ton of stuff. She'd say "I'm not even looking, just go, take it." She enabled us. I took thousands of dollars worth of beanie babies and gifts. I sold a lot of things at a discount and made some extra money.

I became friends with the manager of the clothing store

where I worked. I mentioned the situation at the gift shop and then we started stealing clothes from our store. We hated the company because we felt we were being unjustly treated. They expected us to do things besides retail sales like change light bulbs and go up on high ladders. We also worked very long hours with no breaks–hardly even bathroom breaks. We were understaffed and felt the clothes were overpriced.

We created a scheme we called "The Heist" where we stole huge amounts of clothing. We did it on Sundays when the District Manager wasn't in. The store was usually dead when we did it. We stole anything we wanted. We'd put the clothes in bags and have someone come and take them out. Sometimes, we'd take them ourselves–10 to 15 bags apiece. We took the sensors off as if they were purchased. We never sold the clothes, we wore them ourselves. We were never caught but I ended up leaving both jobs because I needed to make better money. It was hard giving up the stealing but I returned to shoplifting on occasion from both stores. *Either way, it's the feeling of being able to get something for nothing, something that they had but not have to pay for it.*

Soon afterwards, in 1996, I stopped talking to my mother. She had gone to Israel to see my grandfather. He told me he had money for me and my Mom would give it to me. But when she came home, she told me he didn't give her any for me. I found $10,000 in cash and took about $5,000. I took a trip to Chicago with a friend and did other stupid things with the money. She found out and was so angry with me. She broke into my apartment and took things of mine. She took these silver certificates my uncle had given me and some jewelry. Then she told me she would never ever talk to me again. And she didn't.

Around this time I also began stealing more from people which, I feel embarrassed to admit–was always my favorite kind of theft. Shoplifting and employee theft used to be exciting but when I steal from a particular person there was a heightened satisfaction, a rush I'd get that I didn't get from other kinds of theft. A lot of the people I've stolen from were really wealthy. They always seemed to have everything or were giving things to their kids. I was angry, jealous. I always figured they'd never miss it, they'd never know I took it, and that I deserved it, too. It wasn't that I wanted them to feel pain or deprivation except in a couple of instances.

I had one friend who had kids and smoked pot all the time. I didn't think that was good, so I stole from her because I wanted to get back at her. I stole from their purses at parties or public places. I'd never steal a whole purse or wallet because I didn't want them to be without but I wanted the money. My heart would palpitate almost like a panic attack but it was a high.

I knew, especially among friends, when a purse or wallet would be left out. I'd manipulate and lie to get up and check out the scene at their homes. I was never caught but always had an excuse in case someone did catch me. I'd always take the wallet out of the purse and into the bathroom, check it for money and take it, and then put the wallet back in the purse after I'd left the bathroom–that way I'd never really be caught red-handed.

After I stole money, I'd usually go out and buy stuff with it, bring it home, open it up, and lay it all over my bed. I felt a strange pride over what I had done but I was secretly disgusted with myself. The ironic thing is I'm sure any of my friends would have given me any amount of money I wanted or needed–if I had only asked.

I believe I was stealing from good friends who had become like family. Since I used to steal from my Mom but was no longer talking to her, I was acting my feelings out on these other people and somehow rationalizing it–risking abandonment if I were caught. I probably was trying to get back at my own parents and how I was treated in life, how I was robbed from. I wanted to get back at somebody.

Here I was, in my late 20's and early 30's and I knew most people were able to go about their daily lives fairly normally but I couldn't. All I was thinking about was the next time I could steal and who I could steal from, and what day of the week it would be, and how much money I could get. Stealing became my life and my obsession.

I tried to talk myself out of stealing many times but I always felt if I did stop it I wouldn't be able to survive financially on my own. I always justified and a rationalized my behavior. I also overcompensated for my stealing by over giving and being over-generous with friends–often, with the money I had stolen from them.

I continued to work different jobs–babysitting, office work, car valet–but nothing that well-paying or long-lasting. Then, a few years ago, I landed my best job ever as an office manager for a doctor. A friend introduced me to him. About a year later, I found out about C.A.S.A. through a segment on the TV news. I couldn't believe there was a group for people who also had issues with stealing. I began attending immediately. Things were looking up in my life.

Then, in early 2003, my mother died. I didn't even hear about the funeral until well after it had occurred. My brother didn't tell me. He stopped talking to me the same time my Mom did. He was very upset I took money from her. She had cancer and other health issues but I think what really killed her was her anger.

Around this time I began stealing from my boss. It continued for about a year until I was fired. I used office supplies for personal use but he didn't care about that–that was in the open. I abused my phone privileges, too; I was on the phone a lot with friends. He never told me I couldn't do that but it was obvious. I also stole time–I was out of the office

16

constantly, especially when he was gone on Tuesdays and Fridays. I also used his office for my own business purposes. He knew and didn't want to charge me but I started to work while on the clock for him. I wasn't honest about that. I guess I started to feel I deserved the money.

I never thought I would steal from him because he was so giving and loving. We became very close as friends but I got upset with some of his business decisions. He'd let people walk all over him and, I guess, I was going to do the same thing. I felt like he poorly managed his business and had resentments toward him. I tried to help him but he never would change. Everyone tried to help him but he'd do the same thing over and over. It was like in my family because I looked to him as a father figure. He helped me with so many things but it was never enough.

In one case, a lawyer owed him thousands of dollars. I prepared a 20-page letter of itemized expenses. I told my boss not to buckle and to refer the attorney to me but he didn't. Then I started stealing money to make up for the time I had to send out the letters to the attorney and others. As I learned the business, I began to find other loopholes: I'd start taking checks that were sent to the office for depositions and from insurance companies; I'd forge my boss's signature and deposit them into my bank account.

Though I had been attending C.A.S.A. regularly and had admitted stealing from friends, I was too ashamed to admit I'd been stealing from work. By late 2003, I'd graduated from a trade school, completed a personal growth weekend, and met a new boyfriend. I hadn't had a real relationship in over seven years and neither had he. I'd begun to feel hopeful again.

But my world would come crashing down.

It was discovered that I'd been stealing from work. A client was in the office and someone mentioned we hadn't been paid. She said she had paid us. She brought back the cancelled check and there was my name on the back of it. My boss didn't believe it at first and he confronted me and I lied to him. I told him maybe it was an accident and that I'd pay it back. He asked me if there were other checks I'd cashed and I told him "no." Then I had to admit it.

Before I knew it, it was $15,000. I've heard stories of people who've embezzled more than that; but, for me, it was a tremendous amount–half my yearly salary. I thought I'd only stolen about half of that because I kept records. But after a full audit they found it all. In the end, I must have wanted to get caught because I was so stupid and brazen.

When my boss told me he had to fire me it was one of the worst, most humiliating days of my life. My boss had trusted me on so many levels. I betrayed him. I hurt him. I hurt his family. We were a family in that office–me, my boss and his wife. They really trusted me and loved me. I screwed that up. I lost that.

My firing was the real bottom for me. Although they were angry, it was remarkable that they didn't judge me. We had a therapy session together. He told me he didn't want to prosecute but if I couldn't pay him back, he'd have to file a theft claim with the bank and they would likely prosecute me. After my firing, I worked odd jobs and barely made enough money to pay my bills. Somehow, I bought some time and eventually a friend loaned me a chunk to give him. I am paying my friend and my boss back on a payment plan.

My boyfriend has stayed by my side–he's in recovery, too. My closest friends did find out about my firing–some through the grapevine, some I've told myself. Most have been very supportive and understanding of my stealing addiction. Miraculously, my boss and his wife have forgiven me. We've even gotten together for dinner a couple of times. I'm doing better now financially and emotionally. I've continued in therapy and with C.A.S.A.

I haven't stolen anything from anybody in nearly two years but did have a slip a few months ago when I stole an ornate spoon from a friend's sister's home. I was angry with the way she was treating my friend and, I admit, I wanted her to miss that spoon. I decided to mail it back to her anonymously. I still have to keep an eye on my anger. It's likely going to be a lifelong journey.

I call myself a thief and I will always be a thief. I say that because I don't want to ever forget. I don't want to ever go back to that. By saying "I am a thief"–it actually frees me. I know I used to steal from almost anyone, anytime, anyplace. Not anymore. Interestingly, I'd never steal from anybody who I thought didn't have any money or who was in need. I'd never steal from anybody who already knew I was a thief–because then they'd know I did it.

I am grateful for how far I've come in my recovery. I'm no longer ashamed of what I've done, of who I am. I no longer lie to anybody. I'm out with my friends. However, I still haven't told any of them that I have stolen from them, too. I am too afraid they would never forgive me and would leave me. I feel like a real person, a whole person. I used to think I was an imposter. I don't feel like that anymore. I'm human and I've made some mistakes but I've forgiven myself for what I did. I've made amends, I'm making amends.

If I don't go back to stealing, I will be okay. Sometimes bad things lead to good things. I worried I wouldn't be able to survive financially but I'm making more money now than I ever had–from my own business, being my own boss–and by not stealing. The more I give, the more I receive. A lot of people have been on my side and I'm grateful. Stealing was a part of my life that will always be with me but now I know how to deal with it properly. I want to move forward with my life. Through love, I will get better.

Notes & Reflections:

_____

_____

_____

_____

_____

_____

_____

_____

_____

_____

_____

_____

_____

_____

_____

_____

_____

_____

_____

_____

_____

_____

_____

Dave's Story

Dave is a married man, in his mid-thirties, who has made a career for himself in the military. He is reserved and soft-spoken and considers himself to be loyal and spiritual.

I grew up learning it was OK to steal, that it was also fun. My mom would laugh when she stole steak knives from restaurants and would open packages of pens in supermarkets to write the checks. My father worked for a coffee shop/restaurant delivery company. He'd steal and bring home food, coffee, first aid kit stuff. It wasn't an issue.

Once in a while we'd go to my grandparents' house. We'd play this game where we'd sneak stuff out of the garage and put it in the car without grandma seeing us through the window. It was stuff that had "fallen off the truck," like 10 down sleeping bags. Grandpa was a truck driver. My uncle would come by with computers that "fell off the truck." Before you knew it, ten "hot" computers were in the house. I think we kept one; I don't know where the others went.

I also used to go through my Mom's purse and take change from it to buy candy. Sometimes my friends and I would go to the corner market and steal it. My friends would stuff my jacket pockets in the grocery store and I'd be the one holding the stuff on the way out. My "lucky jacket" had a hole in the pocket so the entire lining was open for goodies. We'd have so much candy we'd fill a grocery bag full. Sometimes we'd eat it in a tree out by the back field. Life was good. Good friends. Good times.

Soon I had learned how much of a good time–and a good friend–I had in stealing. Whenever things got crazy or hard, I'd take my bike to go to the store and steal. I even made lists. I stole lots of office supplies–I guess I was priming to steal from work later on.

I got good at stealing. By the time I was ten, I could hold two of the same items and slip one in my pocket without being noticed. I could remove an item from its packaging, right off the rack. I was like a magician. *I was great.*

But, eventually, I got caught. I was tagging along shopping with my uncle and mean Aunt Gloria. We made several stops including at a boating store. I guess she saw I was walking funny. She searched me and found some boat labels and batteries I didn't even need. She took me back to the store managers. They gave me a verbal scare but it didn't seem to phase me completely–I still stole now and then.

About two or three years later–in my mid teens–I got caught again. I'd been store-hopping with my bike and backpack. I'd gone to K-mart and stole some bike supplies. I went to another store and stole some 1984 Olympic pins. I made sure to get one of each kind. A security guard nabbed me. He took a photo of me and all my stolen bounty. He made a comment about how good I was, how sly and sneaky. Though I'd been caught, I felt complimented.

The police arrived and took me to the station until my Dad showed up. They showed me the cell they said they should have put me in for the night to teach me a lesson. I didn't learn my lesson. Where was this big lesson I was supposed to learn? I was put on probation and did some community service. I fixed bicycles with the police explorers for 10 hours. I also did five or six counseling sessions with some guy but continued to steal. He made me draw pictures and punch a heavy bag. It seemed like a waste of time.

Not long afterwards, I stole some valuable coins from my Dad's coin collection and went up to the corner store to play video games. What a jackass I was. Those would have been mine someday. When my family found the coins missing they confronted me and I told them what I did. The store wouldn't even return the coins. To make matters worse, later that day I found out my Dad had been laid off from his steel worker job. My ass hurt so badly from his leather belt, it was incredible. I'm sorrier today than I was then. Those coins were a connection to my grandpa and my Dad; I lost them in the slot of some stupid video game.

After high school, I joined the military; that hardly deterred my stealing either. While on active duty in Hawaii, I stole a check from a roommate I hated. I forged his name, cashed it, and traded for a camera and some smokes (his brand). I sent the camera in the mail to myself at my parents' house in California. Had I not brought it back to Hawaii I probably would've been safe; stupidly, however, I did. Within a week, I was caught up in an investigation. I confessed and lost a rank, received restrictions, and had to pay back the money for the camera. I had the nerve to convince the investigators that since I paid money to the guy I bought the camera from that it was mine. They let me keep it–a small victory.

Next, I was stationed in Italy. My urge to steal was quite strong while I was there. I stole stamps and other supplies while on duty. Once, they searched the whole base but couldn't find the $30 worth of stamps I'd stolen. I was such a good sneak they never found my hiding spot. I even stole cash out of the Chief's locker. They threatened to bring in the investigators. They offered an amnesty but a guard was hovering over the "amnesty spot." The night before, I soaked the money in baby oil and hung it up to dry in the bathroom to get rid of my fingerprints. The next day, I wrapped it up in something and dropped it in the box in a quick, fluid motion. It felt good to be free. Everyone talked about what a sneaky way it was returned.

My life progressed into even more stealing. I kept chasing the excitement of it. The only thing I wanted to get better at in my life was stealing.

I'd married an Italian girl I met there and moved back to the States with her. She really missed her homeland and her huge family who treated me well. Our marriage was horrible. She did nothing for it either. She went to school and met another Italian and became best friends.

I felt rejected. I stole whenever I wasn't with her. I did it all: switched price tags, committed credit card fraud, you name it. I had a price gun, and wasn't afraid to use it. The power of creating my own "fair" prices was immense. Stuff for me, stuff for her, stuff for her niece and nephew. She loved to shop, I loved to shoplift. I did it daily for several years. Then I crossed a line again and stole cash from her Italian friend. Within weeks I confessed and returned the money.

Eventually, I saw the writing on the wall and knew I had to change. I went on a personal growth retreat sponsored by the military chaplain corps. I came back a changed man. I felt I'd gotten over my past but also needed to confront it. I wanted my Mom, my Dad, and my grandpa to admit what they had taught me to do. How could you teach a kid to steal and shoplift? I tried to explain my stealing problem but they didn't get it. Recently, on the phone with my Mom, she joked about having stolen a steak knife from a restaurant. It felt like everything I'd expressed was for naught.

I admit–I blamed my stealing on my parents and my sister because they thought they were better than me. But for the first time in my life I realized whatever I did from this point forward was my own doing. I still can't say for sure what things in my home I bought or stole. *It makes me sick today.*

But despite my best intention to quit, my stealing escalated. I became more brazen then ever. I was at Sears and had bought a 12 volt drill and left but returned to steal an 18 volt drill. I thought I was clear but they were watching. I was detained but then took off running like a crazy man. I ditched half my clothes in the parking lot and ran all over town to evade them. I thought it had worked. I even took a cab home, changed clothes, and came back later to get my car.

About a week later, a sheriff knocked on my door on Sunday morning. Someone must have taken down my license plate. I lied to my wife about it but she found out and our marriage was pretty much over. It was the best thing to happen to me.

I was prosecuted, had to shell out lawyer's fees, and lost eight month's military pay–in addition to pay I lost due to the delay of my pending promotion. I also had to pay for the plane ticket for my ex-wife to return to Italy. I credit my boss for saving my military career, maybe even my life. He encouraged me to get help and the chaplain stood by me, too. I was lucky I wasn't dishonorably discharged.

A few years passed and I wouldn't say I never stole but it was greatly reduced. Then I met my future wife. We've had our ups and downs and I stole while with her as well. But we each found God–on separate time frames. The military pastor married us in a quiet ceremony in my friend's basement. We both wore jeans and were surrounded by close friends. Despite being newly religious and newly married, I began stealing again. I couldn't seem to shake this behavior.

I was even caught by my wife; somehow, she has stuck by me. My greatest fear was being found out. But I'd grown tired of living a secret life. I began meeting with friends in a small Bible study group–a "life group." As I started to share my illness with others, I was met with support and love. They shared a few addictions of their own.

A story from the Bible sealed the deal from me. It spoke to my soul: "For my greatest growth came, when I let go of control of my life and let my Creator take the reins for a while: Yes, I want to be well. I want to be well." I still want to be well. I started my journey with counseling at a Christian counseling center. I had a good perspective on my life even when things were going wrong in my marriage and life. I was with this counselor for about a year. We had made great progress but I needed more expertise when it came to stealing which I finally realized was an addiction.

I went on the Internet and came across a web site and saw I was not alone. I came to know of the founder of the Detroit area support group C.A.S.A. By divine happenstance, my job took me through Michigan into Wisconsin later that summer, 2003. I stopped along the way to get some therapy with Mr. Shulman. I dedicated enough money to fund my "Wellness Trip." I stayed in a nice hotel down the street and pampered myself. I ate well and took care of myself. I spent some heavy duty time with him and came away with some very good tools to stop stealing. I learned how I got to where I am today and where I should be headed. Lucky for me, his wife was a massage therapist who also became an amazingly wonderful, healing person in my life.

Toward the end of my three days of treatment, I was walking outside to get some fresh air. Slowly, I felt raindrops start to fall. *It was magical, spiritual.* The spirit inside of me moved. I felt loved. I felt God's love cleansing me with tears of joy. It was powerful. I stood in the rain and experienced it fully. I knew I needed a good cleansing.

I lost a lot of my good life moving here to Michigan. I lost my men's group. I lost frequent visiting with my grandson, Shawn. I lost my pastor–at least in the flesh. I was on my own. I even thought my wife would never join me in Michigan at my new job. But a year ago, she did. I am now finding more here than what I lost.

I still have temptations to steal. And I've slipped up now and again. I've had my spurts of stealing. I just caught myself spending too much money on stuff–and that's a warning sign. I'll be leaving again soon for another stint with my Unit so I can save my money again. But this disease–or whatever you call it–can only be tackled one day at a time.

I got a couple of "good karma rewards" recently. I bought a certain brand combo drill. It was in an opened box and was missing a battery. I was able to use a rebate form that came with it (on the last day of offer) to get a free jigsaw; and with a missing battery, I got 30% off. Then they found the missing battery hidden in the box but let me have it. A week later, I got a letter from Arby's Restaurant–I'd won a free digital camera for taking a goofy photo at work for some contest. Soon after that, I won a free jump drive for my computer and saved $50 on another great deal. Now I feel I'm rewarded by not stealing–when I do the right thing.

I've been listening to some spiritual CD's again and realize how insane my thinking can be sometimes–doing the same thing over and over in the same way, expecting different results. That's insane. Now, I'm doing things out of my comfort zone–things that are good for me. I don't want to ruin my life. I was digging my own grave and didn't even know it. Addictions are easy to grab, hard to let go of.

I could always find lots of reasons to steal. Now I've been finding reasons not to. It's hard at times but I only have to not steal for today. Sometimes that means not going anywhere by myself. Sometimes it means holding my wife's hand while we're shopping, or sticking close by her side.

Stealing has been a part of me and I have to own that. I've taken risks by telling people–people I love–and it's paid off. I recently told my friend at work and he admitted he went through the same thing. We're both struggling to re-connect with God and we're both honest about our lives.

All I need to do is "plug in" to help myself and do better today than yesterday or, at least, do nothing to hurt myself today. I'm doing well and I don't want to wreck it. I need God back in my life to have clarity and a focused mind. I need to realize I am already the man I need to be–instead of pressuring myself to be the man I think is expected of me.

Notes & Reflections:

Betty's Story

Betty is a Midwestern woman in her 40's, from a small town. She contacted me earlier this year after searching for help for chronic embezzlement from her jobs.

Betty is currently an Executive Director of a Retirement Center. She has a background in accounting. Over the course of just a few years, she embezzled nearly $60,000. Her employer has no idea. Eventually, the stress of her secret life escalated and she confessed to her husband, Frank. She felt suicidal and wound up in a psychiatric unit, experiencing anxiety attacks. She began medication and started to think more clearly, including about her need for real help this time. By the time she had contacted me, she realized she was out of control, unable to stop stealing for very long on her own and wanting to resolve some related underlying issues.

Frank had been through this with her before. A few years prior–as Director of another retirement home–Betty had embezzled nearly $30,000. She had not been discovered but her mounting guilt caused her to confess to her employer. Miraculously, they neither fired her nor pressed charges. She repaid the money through a loan she accepted from Frank, a prominent businessman. Betty left the job a year later. Frank admitted he enabled her by helping her out–especially by not upholding her repayment to him. He became resentful.

Betty describes herself, matter-of-factly, as a very caring and competent person and employee. In her job positions, she's had easy access to checks that come into the business. She embezzled by signing them over and converting them to her own use. She hid this over time by transferring funds around.

Ironically, Betty revealed she rarely spent any of the money on herself; rather, she spent it on others, particularly her husband. Most of her embezzlement began after her current marriage. She'd been married previously but had no such problems. Betty was not your typical thief. She had no other addictions. She was not greedy or materialistic; to the contrary, she over gave in her work life and her personal life.

When Betty and I started our work together, she was racked with guilt. She just wanted to walk into her workplace and confess everything. She had confessed at her previous job but only after she had the money in hand to pay it back. This time she'd embezzled twice as much and didn't know if she could get a loan again. And this time, she and Frank were friends of the owners of Betty's company. Somehow, this made it even harder to tell. She figured even if she was fired or went to jail, anything would be easier than living with the lies and daily torment of working where everyone thought the world of her–if only they knew.

I suggested she and Frank talk about what was best for both of them. Betty wanted relief but, more than anything, she wanted Frank's love and respect. She thought if she confessed to her employer she could also earn back Frank's love and respect. But Frank saw it a different way. As much as he understood her inclinations, he truly feared their life would be ruined–their life–not just hers. Betty didn't want to hurt Frank anymore than she already had. I asked them to consider some of the possible scenarios that could take place.

They described a best case scenario like this: Betty confesses to her employer who is sympathetic to her problem and forgives her, allowing her to pay the money back over time. But, for various reasons, when Betty and Frank stopped to think about it, this was not a very likely outcome this time.

They described a worst case scenario like this: Betty confesses to her employer who fires and prosecutes her and word gets out in their small community. "What else?" I asked Betty. "I'd lose my marriage and ruin my husband's life, too." This may not happen but it, too, was a risk. I asked her if she deserved that kind of fate and punishment; she was on the fence. Did Frank? "Definitely not," she said. Further, I asked Betty to consider other consequences. What if she was beaten, raped or contracted HIV in prison? Was she prepared–as a convicted felon–for possibly never working a decent job again? There was a lot to think about.

After a couple of weeks of discussion, Betty and Frank decided they would take out a loan together and that Betty would secretly repay it over a six month period. Frank would manage all the household bills and Betty would turn her paychecks right over to him to repay the loan.

After two months of therapy with me, Betty had an epiphany while on a recent visit with her husband to see her mother out of state. She realized how much alike these two important people are. Betty came to realize her stealing and over giving was connected to her mother's abandoning her when she was 12 years old. "My Mom left us for a man with a lot of money. I've always had in my mind that if you wanted to keep somebody you'd have to give them a lot. I started to shoplift and steal as a young child and teenager. I remember stealing an expensive blouse for my Mom, hoping to keep her from leaving us." Marrying Frank–whose personality and mannerisms reminded her of her mother–likely triggered Betty's unconscious abandonment issues.

Betty also related how secrets and guilt played a role, too. "We grew up pretty poor and moved around a lot. When I was 4 or 5, my Dad was fired from his job, I think for stealing. My Mom abused my brothers. My family was full of secrets. Everything in my life was a lie. My Mom cheated on my Dad; somehow, I felt it was my fault."

Further, Betty mentioned her father died about 8 years ago, forcing her to return from a good life on the West Coast. He'd been taking care of his mother prior to his death. Betty felt obligated to take that duty after he died. She repressed her anger and stress over this, thus creating feelings of entitlement for her difficult sacrifices. It's no coincidence she has found herself in the line of work she's in.

Frank came to understand why Betty had been so on edge most of their relationship, so distant, so focused on gift-giving. He felt hopeful to find help available for people like Betty. Betty felt relieved to have everything out in the open with Frank and to hear him say he'd stand by her–even during tough times. This kind of unconditional love is what she'd been looking for all her life. As with many crises, people can be brought closer and made more whole.

Betty's path is a long one. She has been on our e-mail support group and has found she is not alone. She has no desire to steal from work and hasn't done so since she confessed to her husband several months ago. It is still awkward for her to work at the company but it is becoming easier. She was offered a promotion which she might have taken except she would no longer have access to money to discreetly pay it back. It remains unclear if she will leave her job after she pays back the all the money. She, of course, will discuss all options with Frank.

In the meantime, she is working on not giving so much at her job and to her husband. She's focused on doing her job well and being "naturally" friendly to her clients and co-workers. She admits she had an almost "Jesus-like" compulsion to touch every resident's hand before she left work which came from a need to overcompensate for her guilty actions and feelings rather than sincere caring and compassion. Betty sees a path now to heal old wounds and also to learn how to live and to love in the present.

Notes & Reflections:

Scott's Story

Scott is a sharp-dressed, 34 year old divorced father of two. He is a former high school teacher who is serving nearly two years in a work release program for criminal matters, including theft. He has been attending CASA over a year.

The first time I remember stealing was when I was about 11 years old. During this time my family was in disarray on its way to disaster. We had just moved from a small town in Northern Michigan to Dallas for my Dad's work. My brother took the move horribly since he was going into high school at that age. I saw it more as an adventure for me. My brother got in with the wrong crowd and started rebelling. Things in our family really fell apart.

My half-brother, who was 15 at the time, sent me in a store to steal a container of chewing tobacco and he waited outside. I never asked him why he didn't just do it on his own, probably because he thought if I got caught they'd let an 11-year old go but maybe not a 15-year old. I got caught and they took me into this room. They tried to call my parents but they weren't home. I was petrified about what my Dad would do to me. I begged them to let me go; eventually, they did. I didn't steal again for a short while.

I was the kid who always got away with everything. I knew how to spin words and charm adults from an early age. I was the golden child. In my early teens, I began stealing on my own–this was fueled by the deep conviction that no matter what kind of trouble I might get into, I'd always find a way out of it, there'd be minimal trouble, I'd always come out with my head above water. My brother hated responsibility and passed it on to me even though I was the little brother. I loved taking on responsibility in whatever form.

34

We moved back to Michigan from Texas around the time I was in junior high. By then, I had started to dabble around with shoplifting, mostly cassette tapes. In seventh grade, I got caught taking a cassette from a Meijers store. My parents didn't make a big deal out of it. They looked the other way, thinking that's probably typical 13-14 year old behavior. But I was already learning how to push things to the edge. I took every yard when I was given an inch–in all my behaviors.

By junior high I was trying to keep up with the cool kids I wanted to be friends with. They had nice clothes, their parents had lots of money–they had this and that. At some point, I realized I could just get anything I wanted for free.

In the '80's–especially in Northern Michigan–there was no security; there were no cameras, no beeper systems that went off. Stealing was a piece of cake. You just went in and–if you could conceal it–there was no problem. I had the attitude "I'm gonna get what I want and if I do get caught I'll find a way out of it." It was addictive, powerful–that feeling of getting whatever I wanted when I wanted it–the Ralph Lauren Polo clothing, the things other kids had. I didn't have to ask Mom or Dad for money.

Stealing brought more of a sense of accomplishment than a rush or a high. I don't recall enjoying the feeling while I was in the act. It wasn't until I got home and lay the clothes on the bed that I realized how much I had just gotten for free. That was the rush. I actually hated the feeling of my heart pounding and the adrenaline rushing through me and the fear of getting caught. There were many times I'd have to take a deep breath after leaving the store just to get my center. But the feeling of getting four shirts–anything I wanted– was the addiction, the getting something for nothing, for free.

I always knew right from wrong because I grew up with that. I went to private schools and my parents did their best to teach me morals. But, somehow, that all got lost as I saw in society and all around me–people cheating on their taxes, people doing all kinds of things to bend the rules. I must have thought things through and justified it. Many times I thought to myself "this is getting out of hand." I'd slow down, get scared, or feel an extra sense of guilt.

But my stealing became brazen and very frequent. My life was at a difficult stage. I felt lost: no job, a tenuous sense of home, and little real self-worth. I was going three to five times a week to stores to shoplift. It wasn't just a spur of the moment thing–I'd plan out what I'd want to get.

I always shoplifted alone and never sold anything I stole. I gave many things away as gifts to friends or family. Maybe I felt less guilty that way. Christmas time–that was big–why not? I'd load up at Christmas. Even in recent years–in my late 20's and early 30's–I shoplifted more for others, like my kids. I stole clothes for my wife so she wouldn't spend our money. She'd want to go out and spend $300 on clothes but I'd go steal $300 worth of clothes. I hated spending money on anything I could steal.

Periodically, people around me wondered where I got all these things. My Mom–in high school and college–used to ask me where I got all my clothes. "I borrowed it from a friend," whatever. What's she gonna say? She could have called a friend to check. But I worked good jobs during the summer and my parents never kept tabs on how much money I had. Looking back on it, they were more concerned than they led on. They probably fell into that trap a lot of parents fall into–they don't want to think or believe their kid is doing something wrong. My ex-wife used to wonder, too, but she probably enjoyed the things I brought home too much.

I seemed to need the sense of accomplishment I seemed to get from stealing. For some reason, I had insecurities and really sought out approval. I constantly compared myself to others and felt this need to compete, especially with what they had. In college, I stole 3, 4, 5 CD's a week. I had over 900 of them; 85-90% of them were stolen. In my fraternity, I had more music than anyone else. People knew when they wanted a particular disc, they came to me. It's those subtle things: I'm important because I have all the music or other little gadgets, video games, whatever.

I made myself feel important in a very fake way. I'd have good things, cool things. I didn't see I should just be what I am. When I was young, I didn't think like that. It's a mature thought to accept that some people like you for who you are and some won't–and that's okay. I needed to be accepted: being the kid who lived on the edge was how I got accepted.

I don't know why I developed such insecurities and such a need for approval. I've examined it have a couple of theories. One, I was always held to high expectations. I remember my grandma saying "I know Scott's going to be a doctor." I was the first of her grandchildren to go to college. Even my parents always had this thing about me that I was really going to achieve a lot. I think, subconsciously, it was a lot to live up to. The reality was I was a very average person.

With athletics, I was small. As a freshman in high school, I weighed 105 pounds. I had to fight to prove I was good enough and strong enough. The minute I faced any hurdle that made things hard to achieve, I'd get down on myself for failing and I didn't want to let others down.

In academics–this goes hand-in-hand with stealing–I cheated a lot. I didn't have to. I got good grades. But when it got difficult, I was afraid to get a B and not an A. I needed a guarantee I'd do okay even if I stumbled a bit–I could fall back on a "cheat sheet." I even sold my own answers to other kids. I figured I wasn't cheating–they were.

When I look back on my life, so much of it was based on cheating: cheating on how I got things, cheating on how I portrayed myself to other people. This probably just reinforced my poor sense of self. I feared failing, not achieving. I also feared the effort it took to do things the right way. I don't know why.

Besides shoplifting and cheating, I began stealing from work as a senior in high school. I worked at a sporting goods store the start of my senior year during football season. I stole little things like gloves you'd wear to play football in the cold weather, some shoes, whatever. Then I got a job at a restaurant. I learned to scam cash as a waiter, especially when people ordered drinks or paid in cash. It would be so easy to pocket it. I'd give them their bill–which might be $150–and they'd look it over and give me the cash. Then I'd delete one of the entrees–the official register might say $125 but they'd already seen the bill for $150 so I could pocket an extra $25. I stole hundreds and hundreds of dollars.

When I got my first real job–as a high school teacher–I had a key to the storage area. I'd get myself extra cokes and other thing. I didn't steal any big items like computers or things like that. But everywhere I looked, I found I needed to scam something, even if it was just a candy bar. It became so addictive–so part of me–that the first thing I'd do anytime I walked into a room or a new environment was to scan and instantly look for what I could take–be it a 12-pack of coke, a tray of food, or three items for the price of two.

When I got married in '95 my life took a big change. I looked at putting an end to my stealing and scamming ways. I don't know how it happened but it was like how I just quit drinking after college. Now I was married and responsible and went to work to support my new wife and a five-month old baby from the marriage she'd just left.

I toned it down. But every now and then I'd still shoplift. If something on the car broke–I'd steal a part so I didn't have to spend the money. When money got tight in the marriage I realized I could steal groceries. I'd steal $200 worth of groceries by just walking in with bags from the store and cleverly fill up a cart. Sometimes I'd put like a big roll of paper towels over the stuff in the cart to hide it. But I always believed if you just acted like you're not doing anything wrong, people don't take notice. You just do your shopping and walk out the door. If your stuff was in bags and people are looking, they're going to think you paid for it.

I also felt great pressure from my wife to buy nice things, to have the money to get what we wanted–brand names. She made me feel "less than" if I said "we can't afford it." I liked nice things, too, but I hated spending the money. I even hated spending money on things like diapers and toiletries–I'd rather use the money to go out for dinner or something.

My marriage began to deteriorate and I was unhappy in my career. My whole perception of life changed and my stealing escalated. The beginning of the end for me was when my marriage finally fell apart. I just stopped caring about everything. I just stopped caring about my life. I took the easy way out: I had an affair with a woman at my work. I was letting life dictate its terms to me instead of making decisions about my life. I wasn't choosing fully to steal or not steal. I wasn't choosing fully to be in a career that excited me. I wasn't choosing fully to stay in or leave my marriage. The big thing was: how does it look on the surface to everybody else?

I got back into alcohol and, later, drugs. It seemed like a good idea to me to party more and act like it was all okay. I felt like I was having more fun in my life but I really wasn't. I had a boat and the next thing you know I'm partying on the lake. I was drinking on a regular basis, then someone was offering a joint, and then people had cocaine. Soon I was doing both. I knew where I could get the stuff and a month or two later I'm bringing cocaine to the people on the lake. It was the same old thing: now I'm important because I've got something people want. Everybody loved me. My drug use went from just a weekend thing to using during the week.

One night I was out with my wife and some friends. She was ready to go home and go to bed. I had to stay out late with my friends–if you can call them that. At four in the morning I was pulled over by the cops. I'd been drinking; they searched the car and found the drugs. I got a DWI and a possession charge. The only good news was that this all happened early rather than later because it was easier to quit. I never expect to do drugs again.

I was convicted on the DWI and drug possession and lost my job as a High School teacher and coach. I had gotten a break by getting hired in the first place because I had a criminal record of theft. They had viewed it as a sign of immaturity when I was hired in '96. My arrest was in the paper and then–on top of that–the press did a little digging and found out about my past criminal record of theft. This put pressure on the school to explain why they had hired me in the first place even though I had eight years of an excellent teaching record. They fired me and the state revoked my teaching certification. I went to jail for 90 days in the County Jail work release program.

While on work release, I should have evaluated my life and how I got to this point; instead, I tried to repair my image–do the right thing, don't drink or drug, find a new job. None of that stuff mattered. I needed to save me–inside. I never went to therapy or sat down with my parents to tell them I needed help. I got caught up in the superficial again.

When I got out of work release, nothing had changed. I'd met a guy in work release who was doing two weeks for drunk driving and he was a millionaire. He heard my story and said I'd be making more money than I was making as a teacher. I took the job but I didn't learn my lesson. I didn't stop to look at the real problem. I was covering up a wound with a band-aid, thinking it would go away.

I wasn't drinking or drugging but I was still stealing, still feeling like I was garbage. The court and my probation only emphasized my drinking and drugging; nobody addressed my stealing because nobody knew. I hated keeping it a secret but I was too scared and ashamed to reveal it.

Five weeks after I was out of work release, I was still in a marriage I didn't want to be in, living in a community I felt ostracized from, humiliated and embarrassed. My new job didn't go as well as I had hoped in the beginning. Money was tight again. Then my wife started in with "we gotta buy this, we gotta buy that" and I think I cracked. I felt like a big failure all over again. I think I had a slight breakdown.

Next thing you know, I'm in a Meijers store and just loaded up a shopping cart. Instead of shoplifting more safely like I'd always done before, I just started taking all these other things like a mobile phone and a mini-fireplace for the back patio. I had the cart filled head-high. I saw a guy watching me. I saw him watching me and I wheeled the cart right out past the flower landscaping area and the same guy came right out the door–I knew he was watching me. On any other day, I would have just given it up and walked away but I kept going. Fifty feet out the door and he's coming after me with a radio and then there's another guy coming. Here I was stealing more than $500 worth of stuff.

On top of this, prior to going in–I had borrowed my buddy's pick-up truck–I had put a $200 swing for our porch in the back of his truck. I can't explain how careless I was and what I was thinking that day. *People have suggested to me maybe I wanted to get caught–I don't know. But you do get to the point where you know your life is out of control and nothing seems right, nothing makes any sense, so why should my behavior?*

I actually ran from the guy and got away but they saw the license plate on the truck and my buddy was contacted. Then the police contacted me and I tried to make up some story about how somebody else borrowed his truck but none of that was flying. They put a warrant out for me and I got a lawyer after almost killing myself. I thought I was going to go to prison and now I had two young kids. *I felt lower than I'd ever been.* My Dad convinced me to go with him to this lawyer's office and turn myself in. Here I get this brand new felony while I was still on probation.

The judge gave me a year of work release and he was the kind of judge that sends everybody to prison. Now I have to go before the other judge whose probation I violated. Everyone thought I'd be going to prison. The prosecutor was asking for 1-15 years. My wife had filed for divorce and my kids were gone. Most of my friends had given up on me. The other judge also gave me a year of work release but ran it consecutively rather than concurrently, which meant I'd be serving close to two years rather than one. It boiled down to 17 months–I should be out by Christmas Eve.

In a strange way, something good happened. The treatment lady for my new probation took a closer look at my file and noticed a history of theft offenses. She said, "Wait a minute, this doesn't make sense here. You're a well-educated, intelligent person and something's not congruent here. There's a much greater problem going on here." She gave me a number for C.A.S.A. I procrastinated for a couple of weeks before going to my first meeting in July 2004. It has been the missing piece in my road back to sanity.

The last time I stole anything was about a year ago, when I was caught on April 24, 2004. It was my son's birthday party. Now my son's birthday is this Saturday and I'm missing it because I'm in jail on the weekend.

The most important thing I've learned is that all those years I felt out of control and felt I had no choice–it could have been different but I needed help. I isolated myself from everyone– my parents, my friends–because I was afraid of what they'd see. I've learned you have to let people in, you have to ask for help and admit your weaknesses. You have to be able to go to people and say "I'm not doing so well with this." Once I did that and was able to sit down with my parents and friends and tell them all the things I'd been doing wrong, so much pressure fell right off of me.

It's almost scary but it's been easier to get to this stage of recovery than I thought it would be. I thought it would be a lot harder to quit stealing. I'm still facing a lot. I'm still in the work release–if I did something wrong now, I'm going to prison. I think the biggest challenge will be in a couple of years–when I'm off work release and probation. What will happen then if my life takes a difficult turn? Will I go back to stealing? I don't think I will because I have a support group–C.A.S.A.–and I have my parents, friends, and wonderful girlfriend. I have friends who know what's going on and they're here for me; they tell me they're not going to tolerate the same stuff anymore. Most of all, I have my sense of worth now, my pride, my self-love.

I have so much to look forward to. I've avoided prison. I have great kids. Everyday I think of this: "I'm not trying to recover, I'm recovering." It is do or don't do. There's no "trying." I'm going to recover and stop living life looking for cheating angles, looking for the easy road, and I'm just going to do the next right thing. It just makes perfect sense. I have woken up. It's not difficult but it's so difficult when you don't do it with other people. It's good to know people who know what it's like to be addicted to stealing. I know life has to be great because I'm not doing things to make my life worse. Even if I don't achieve some of my goals whether financial or otherwise, I'm not doing anything to make my life worse. I'm headed in the right direction.

Notes & Reflections:

Holly's Story

Holly is a 40 year old artist and bookkeeper for a small design company in the Southwest. She had been a relatively honest person until a little over a year ago when she embezzled $20,000 from work in one year.

Up until recently, I only stole a few minor things as a teenager, nothing out of the ordinary. I was raised by my Dad from the age of two or three after he and my mother divorced. I don't remember much from that time. He remarried when I was eight and I had a fairly normal life with my step family. My Dad was and is an alcoholic but totally functional. He never missed a day of work. He never overtly abused or neglected me but I've begun to see his drinking negatively affected me in ways. I dated a man for three years and then we were married for another three. He was an abusive alcoholic. I don't have children.

I was an academic overachiever in high school and was involved in a lot of activities. I went to college but didn't last very long. I went back after my divorce and became an overachiever again–this time in graphic design. I never graduated–fell short a few credits.

I've made a living doing art work. I moved to this state about five years ago to follow my job. It's hard to believe that in less than a year, I embezzled nearly $20,000 from my work by writing checks to myself from the business check book.

Prior to my embezzlement, I never stole anything else from any workplace. It was a spontaneous act the first time. I had access to the checkbook because it was part of my duty to write checks. I felt under pressure when a roommate moved out and I stole about $1,000 by forging a check I took from the checkbook. I wrote it to myself and signed it. I felt very numb about the whole thing–it was almost like a non-reaction. I'm sure on some level I was mortified but I felt numb completely. I deposited and cashed it. I figured $1,000 would take me out of the momentary financial jam.

Initially, I intended it to be a one time thing–I'm not sure if I was going to keep it or pay it back. I didn't get that far. Almost immediately after the first incident I began thinking "well, maybe I can help get myself out of another jam with maybe a little more, maybe a little more." I embezzled fairly consistently over the next year–about every other week–between $500 and $1,000, some less, some more. I always used the same method and my boss never checked.

However, as time passed, my work suffered severely–both the quality and efficiency. And it wasn't just my work: I kept more secrets and failed to expose minor mistakes or little problems in the office which had nothing to do with me. I failed to tell my boss "there's a little problem here"–I tried to take care of it but really she should have known. I feared any one problem would open up an investigation into what I'd been doing and I'd be blamed for everything. Our friendship suffered as well. I closed down about things in my life–I told myself "that's what you need to do right now."

When I decided to come clean about my stealing and to get help, part of it was that tax time was coming and I knew I'd be found out. Also, one day I just lost it at work when my boss and her accountant unexpectedly asked me why the general ledger was out of balance. I didn't know how to answer. I had tried to balance it but it obviously didn't work. I made an excuse to leave and was gone for three or four days. I'm sure my boss started nosing around to see why I wasn't coming back and discovered the checks I'd written.

I was in panic mode. I searched the Internet for help and found the C.A.S.A. web site. I'd contacted Debtors Anonymous–which didn't seem like the best fit; they didn't return my calls. There was nothing else I felt could help me.

46

My boss left a message on my machine saying "I've found out some things and I want you to come back and help me put this back together." I had only two choices: I could ignore it–but she had enough evidence to prosecute me; or, I could take a risk and trust that she really wanted me to help her put the pieces back together. I knew deep inside what I needed to do–just come clean, no matter what the ramifications were. I called her to say I was coming in.

When I finally met my boss face to face I just broke down in tears. I was shaking. I was terrified the police would be there. I didn't know if I was being reported. I didn't even know how to explain what I had done. All I knew was that I had to somehow try. I told her how I did it and was shocked to find out how much I'd stolen. I thought it was a lot less. I told her I'd do whatever it took to repay her and I respected her decision about what to do–if she decided to prosecute, I wouldn't fight it, I wouldn't run from the law, I'd take what ever punishment there was.

She, of course, asked me "why, why, why?" I tried to explain but I told her I really didn't know why either. I told her my reasons in the moment but not the deeper reasons because I didn't know them yet. I admitted I felt justified on some level to do what I did and I still don't know why that is. Her reaction to all of this was "it's over and if it ends now–if you can make full disclosure and restitution–we'll deal with it on a day by day basis." And that's exactly what we've done over the last six months.

I was amazed she offered that then and I'm amazed now. We've had our ups and downs. There's just the two of us working together. We work in a spiritual environment where we share different perspectives on what's going on and how to handle it. I still work everyday with all the deeper issues that go way beyond the stealing and with honesty and full disclosure of everything that goes on in the office. I'm not taking the control away from her, the employer.

We have some new checks and balances. I showed her everything I did and how I did it. I've helped her put systems in place where–if I'm no longer working for her–others can't steal from her. I've helped her see those windows of opportunities where she is vulnerable to theft. Her son helped us, too. He was upset at what I did but was very non-judgmental. He and my boss know I work hard and do a huge amount of work. In many ways it would have been harder to fire me than keep me. I could imagine her saying to me "please don't leave." I don't think she wanted to lose me. I'd been with her six years and her attitude was "let's see if we can work this out." I don't think I was consciously aware of taking advantage of her reliance on me as a justification for stealing. That whole year I was stealing is still like a blur.

Now, rather than put my energies into new ways to steal, I put them into ways to prevent theft. It's not been easy for either of us because her method of business is based on trust. Previous employees have taken from her. My intention is for me to be the last. They've stolen money and time from her. She fired them and filed charges each time. I guess the difference in my case is I didn't run. I made the choice to come to her–at least after a short hiding out–and said "I did this and whatever you need to do, do." I'd consulted a few lawyers before I confessed and they all said "don't you dare." But I knew I had to. In my mind it wasn't even debatable once I trusted my gut instinct. She took a risk, too, by giving me a second chance to make this right.

I'm paying her back a bit at a time–she's been kind enough to be pretty patient. She's almost like a sponsor helping me budget my money. I report to her on a bi-weekly basis. I'm putting in extra hours at work which is kind of like community service. I put in every extra hour I possibly can to make this better. We have a different relationship now. If there's something even remotely wrong or out of place she'll tell me if she feels I'm not being completely honest. Sometimes, frankly, I have my moments where I'm very offended–I don't have to answer these questions! Yet, this is part of my process of becoming more honest with me and I'm thankful. Otherwise, I do my business as usual.

Over the last six months I've also come to realize some related issues in my life. I've felt victimized, taken advantage of, and betrayed over and over again. My big thing is abandonment; I'm afraid people are going to leave. When I get in that kind of situation I don't handle it well. Whether it was my mother leaving me, my ex-husband abusing me, or my roommate leaving me, I don't handle abandonment well–or what I perceive to be abandonment. Yet, I see the irony: I can push people away faster than anyone in the world. I create every situation to let them leave. And then I tell them "if you can't handle this, you can leave." I'll give them permission to leave, though it's the one thing I don't want them to do. This is all part of my attempt to control the uncontrollable.

I've learned a lot of this from the C.A.S.A. e-mail group and my participation in 12 Step groups. I'm also in therapy but finding it only moderately effective. I get more out of my 12 Step groups–Overeaters Anonymous, Nicotine Anonymous, and Alanon. OA is my primary program but I apply the 12 Steps to any problem in my life and to all my addictions. I'm more than just scratching the surface; I'm taking a shovel to my issues. It feels good.

When I first contacted Mr. Shulman, I had every excuse in the book for stealing–I was short on money because my roommate had just left; my family lived far away and wasn't able to help. Now I see it was all a control game. I like control. And rather than ask for help–which I never did–I just took from those who were closest to me–the nearest, easiest target. Asking for help was a sign of weakness, neediness. My boss and I were fairly close and I feared she'd judge me for not having it altogether financially.

I've also come to recognize I've had a pattern of addictive behaviors in my life prior to stealing. If it's not one thing, it was another. The first addiction I remember having was overeating–that's probably my first and most deeply-rooted addiction.

In the six months since I've come clean I've had no relapses with theft and no real urges to steal. I've had some passing thoughts like "this is the kind of opportunity I used to take advantage of." I try to identify them and work them through in my head by saying to myself "it's not acceptable for me to steal. The only acceptable thing is for me to identify why I'm thinking or feeling a certain way."

Everybody knows what I did–my family, my roommates, my boyfriend–and they're all supportive of me. I felt they needed to know as they're in my life on a daily basis. They felt I did the right thing and I'm glad all the underlying issues have been coming to the surface. They see my stealing as addictive behavior. It was another cry for help. I'm still working on those underlying issues like asking for help, not over achieving, and easing my fears of abandonment. Right now I'm just trying to identify thoughts and feelings and analyze the problem and ridding myself of addictions rather than picking up new ones. I even quit smoking 30 days ago.

I've even thought about what I would have done if I was my boss and the shoe was on the other foot. Honestly, I think I would have done the same thing and given her a chance. If my boss had fired or prosecuted me I don't think I would have gotten the same help. Practically speaking, one of the board members from a business we work with looked me right in the eye and said "you need to get into a 12 Step group and go to 90 meetings in 90 days." I took her advice. She's a psychiatrist. It has turned a lot around for me. I'm grateful people have been firm with me but also caring.

Notes & Reflections:

Rocco's Story

Rocco is a suburban husband and father of two, mid thirties, with an MBA. He has been an assistant manager at a large home wares retailer for the last several years. He has regularly embezzled money and stolen merchandise—mostly to keep or hoard. He's engaged in other forms of theft as well.

Rocco came to see me earlier this year. Several years ago, he had voluntarily attended C.A.S.A. meetings a few times and then stopped. He's had a mental health history of depression and anxiety since his early teens when he experienced some non-violent molestation by a close family member. Later, in his high school years, he was held up at gun point at an ATM. He has suffered PTSD (Post Traumatic Stress Disorder) since that event.

His symptoms have included a blunted emotional affect, restlessness, self-harm behavior (cutting oneself both to numb feelings and to experience or ground feelings), and chronic theft behaviors including shoplifting, employee theft, and taking items from cars, yards, and garages of homes. He had graduated a few years earlier from an out-of-state inpatient self harm program. His wife also knew about his theft behaviors but not to their full extent.

Rocco returned to C.A.S.A. and to see me for therapy within a month of being arrested for breaking into several cars and stealing belongings. He was picked up by the police shortly after the break-ins as he was driving erratically. He was put on a suicide watch at the hospital. If ever a person's actions were a cry for help, Rocco's were. His therapist was out of town and the stresses of work, the Christmas Season, and recently becoming a first-time parent were overwhelming.

During our work together and through his regular attendance at C.A.S.A. we explored the connections between his theft behaviors and his life history. It became clear this mild-mannered man was still intensely hurt and angry about the violations of his boundaries by others. To complicate matters, his wife–a caring yet linear-thinking person–had become more parent than partner, controlling and advising him which felt like a further violation to him. This approach both angered him as well as shut him down.

At his job, as well, Rocco felt underpaid, taken advantage of, and diminished. He didn't care for his line of work but it became familiar and comfortable. He'd long put on the backburner his dream of operating his own landscaping company. His feelings of frustration and victimization would build up and, inevitably, he engaged either in self-harm or theft behaviors. He would usually self-harm after stealing to numb the guilt and shame. His stealing, particularly, was a way of striking back when he felt attacked. For a moment, he felt like he'd gotten back some power and autonomy.

In therapy, I quickly got his wife involved and encouraged her to read my book. She also needed to be educated about theft as an addictive behavior. Rocco, in essence, was using stealing very similar to how an addict uses drugs or alcohol– to cope with life's stresses. Initially, his wife didn't understand this concept. She felt less in the dark after reading my book and coming to C.A.S.A.'s once-a-month family night. This–in turn–helped Rocco feel more understood and more able to speak honestly with her about the extent of his past and present theft behaviors.

As Rocco revealed he'd been stealing from work, his wife naturally became alarmed. His other therapist suggested he quit immediately to avoid temptation and possible firing and prosecution; after all, he had a court case pending on the car break-ins. I could sense Rocco's hesitancy. I had a different suggestion. I acknowledged it was risky to stay at the job but encouraged a more gradual approach. I knew if Rocco left work and had no money coming in and much less structure for his time, his self-harm and other theft behaviors likely would escalate. Ideally, I also wanted to use his work as a testing zone; I had him work on being assertive and speaking up, practicing new coping skills for anger and stress. He began making immediate progress.

We also set modest goals for Rocco to move forward on his landscaping business. Within a few months, he had more jobs than he could handle–mostly from family, friends, and neighbors. He no longer felt trapped at his job. His confidence blossomed.

Along the way, he reported a few relapses into self-harm and theft behavior. His wife felt terrified. She wanted him to return to the out-of-state, self-harm inpatient program. He had promised her several years ago he'd never self-harm again. Without minimizing his relapses, I helped them understand that during times of difficult changes, they are common. I also advised Rocco against making any promises which tend to cause undue pressure and stress. We needed to take things one day at a time.

A month later, Rocco reported he'd not only gone without any self-harm or theft behaviors, but he'd had a monumental and surprising emotional release. One day at work, he began sobbing uncontrollably. He found a safe, quiet space and let it all out. It was as if the ice had melted. He had returned to his real self. I commented how he looked like a completely different person–more present, relaxed, light, and energized. His wife recently told me how much better he was doing.

Rocco now reports he actually feels good about not stealing from work or elsewhere. He admits he still has had temptations but he feels better about himself and thinks more about his future. He plans to gradually wean himself from his job in retail to either landscaping or something else. He and his wife just found out they are expecting another child. This time, he told me, he gets to truly feel the joy he deserves.

Notes & Reflections:

Paul M's Story (A store owner-interviewed in 2003)

Paul is the manager and co-owner of a Midwest independent retail store. He is soft-spoken and sweet but noticeably hardened and bitter. His short story illustrates how real people are adversely affected by shoplifting and employee theft. Regardless of the type or size of the store, the stress on working people is palpable. There are no nameless, faceless entities involved—only real people with real lives.

My father started this business in the 1950's and I've been in it over twenty years now. I'm finding it harder and harder to stay in business and I know I'm not the only one. First, it's getting harder and harder for the little guy, the small businesses, to survive in the world of big businesses, franchises, and conglomerates. That's tough enough. But the other challenge in any business, and this is certainly true with ours, is shrinkage, or loss of product by theft.

It's gotten worse and worse over the years. It's both external losses–shoplifting–but more demoralizing is the internal loss, the employee theft. I was reading a retailer statistic the other day and it stated that both forms of theft have gone up in the last two years since 9/11 with the souring economy. I think the figure for internal loss was more dramatic, something like a 60% increase. I don't doubt it. It's tough. You don't know who you can trust anymore. We've hired friends and family members and even they have stolen. You can't trust anybody anymore. It's sad.

I think it's some kind of entitlement thing with most people, particularly the younger ones who are the people we're most likely to employ. The feeling they seem to have is that stealing isn't wrong, like everybody does it. Sometimes they act on their own but often they do it together. Shoplifting is less of a concern for us than employee theft.

I don't think they get how much it hurts our family, not just financially but emotionally. I mean, some of these kids we watched grow up. We've mentored them, or at least tried to; some of them we've lent money to, helped them out in other ways, we even sent one of them to college. It's heartbreaking. There's hardly a day I don't dread going into work. I'm always on edge–it's bad enough just trying to run a business but to have to watch our own employees? It's not fun. They act like they like you and are loyal to you. We treat them well. We like to think, as a small business, we're a more laid back, more personal, better place to work. I guess it doesn't matter. We've got employee discounts, rewards; we give them store credit, bonuses, gift cards–just to deter them from stealing. Nothing seems to work.

We've discovered so many different schemes, it's amazing. We don't have the best security but we've got some. We do modest background check but we don't have electronic tags or gates. We have some security cameras but those are mainly to watch the employees and we don't monitor the cameras as much as we need to–that would be expensive. We have a multi-story building and we've closed a few of the upper floors–we use them for storage. The employees were dropping merchandise out the windows to people.

Some of our employees get cell phone calls or make calls while on duty. I know some of them use their phones to make calls to each other or to the outside when it's safe to steal, like when I'm busy with a customer. It's crazy. I've tried to ban cell phones from the workplace but there was a big protest. They feel they need their phones for emergencies or feel it's a basic right. I told them I survived without a phone. If they need to be contacted in case of an emergency, someone can call the store phone. The problem I have–which puts me in a bind–is it's hard to find employees to begin with. If I ban the phones or enforce other strict rules, I may not get anyone to work for me.

I've had to drastically downsize the business, partly because of the competition and the economy but also because the more employees I have, the more shrinkage I have. It gets too hard to keep track of 15 employees. Now I'm down to about five. I've considered hiring security guards, installing more sophisticated security systems, doing all the things the big boys do with their stores. But frankly, they spend millions of dollars and I know they still have problems.

It seems the best employees are the ones who steal the most. They learn the system and do great in sales and customer service, they win your trust and appreciation and then they start turning on you. I've had to let so many of those go. It's as if it's better to hire incompetent people because they seem to be less devious.

We have kids who steal from us and have the nerve to wear the clothing to work. It's hard to prove, though. Sometimes they rip the labels off the clothes but that doesn't really do anything except make you more convinced they stole it. And they have a thing about shoes. It's gotten to the point where I have to ask them what size shoes they wear to keep track of what's missing and who likely stole them.

Besides wearing the clothes or using the other stuff they steal, I know for a fact a lot of them are selling what they steal. Once, a customer came back to the store to return something but I ran it through the scanner and there was no record of it being sold. An employee was at the counter and got nervous and tried to take care of it for the customer. That's when I knew. I fired him on the spot. But it's rare you catch someone red-handed.

Once, a friend of mine saw an employee selling our items at a local park. I was out of town and, supposedly, that employee was off sick that day. I had another incident where I was renting out a house of mine to a few long-term employees. I went to the house one day to check on something and found bags full of stuff they'd stolen from the store. I ended up taking the bags and putting the things back on the shelf at the store the next day. It was quite a scene watching them squirm at work that day. They vacated my house that day and I knew they weren't coming back to work or to my house. Later, I found business cards they'd made with my home address right on them! I'm sure there were others that were in on it, too, but I couldn't prove it.

Imagine going to work each day feeling like your employees and co-workers are your enemies. It's awful. I experienced intense depression and anxiety. I had other things going on in my life, too. My mother was dying, my marriage was in trouble. People don't stop to think how their actions are affecting others.

I had let one of my best employees go a while ago. He'd been with us a long time. I didn't catch him red-handed but I know he was stealing. He still comes in every now and then to say hello and I can tell by his questions that he's still trying to figure out why I let him go. It's killing him. It's torture. I just told him at the time it was time for him to grow up and move on; there were better things in store for him.

The reason I don't prosecute is it would take so much time and energy I don't figure it's worth it. Maybe I should. As for the shoplifting, I don't think my employees think that's wrong either. They have a big problem even staying close to the customers; they feel they're smothering them and fear the customers will get upset. I tell them, there's an art to it. We're not a self-serve store. Customers aren't supposed to try everything on and make a mess of the whole store. That's not good business. Then it takes two hours for an employee to straighten up after them instead of assisting them. It's also a deterrent to have an employee nearby as well.

Every now and then we'll bring in a consultant or a detective to hang out for a bit, put the employees on edge. As far as drug testing or other screening, it's hard and expensive to do. I honestly worry we wouldn't find anyone to work here if we asked everyone: have you ever stolen something small from work? I bet almost everybody would flunk that question, especially if we had a polygraph. It's sad.

Paul M's Story (An update interview, June 2005)

Well, it's been two years since we last talked and now there's more shoplifting than employee theft. It seems to go in cycles. I think it has to do with how bad the economy is. People don't have the money and it's too tempting for them. We've also been getting more of an urban crowd as some of our things are now more fashionable.

Another reason employee theft is down is–since we last talked–I've downsized our store space about 25%. Part of that is to keep a better eye on things and part of it is our business is down. We also lost three long-time employees. We tried to keep older people working because they have a better work ethic. They were full-time folks. Now, besides my Dad, I have just a few part-time people. If I have less people to watch they can't say it was the other guy. When we don't have as many employees to watch the customers, the shoplifting goes up. It's a trade-off.

I don't think any of the small retailers like me are going to be in business much longer. It gets harder and harder and you start losing more and more money. There are fewer people who want to work for small companies. And the big guys keep getting bigger. I've been thinking of going to more of an Internet-based business. The only time we really make much of a profit is during the busier times of the year–like the Holiday season. But we have to hire more part-time people during that time and we have more employee theft. It's mostly merchandise because I do not allow access to the cash register.

I've had a few more employees with the gall to open up their own businesses by selling stolen merchandise from my store. I noticed one employee–a week after I hired him–wearing some of our merchandise. I warned him but stupidly gave him another chance. Next thing I found out–he was taking orders from people. He actually had his own business cards made up. I got a call from an anonymous person who tipped me off. It's like a game of cat and mouse. I didn't fire him because I was in a pinch at the time and needed workers.

You have to do a cost-benefit analysis. I have to weigh both sides. You also have to be careful. I just saw an article where an employee who was stealing sued his former employee and won $500,000 because the employer told other employees he'd been fired for theft. It's crazy. Our bottom line is to get rid of them as quick as I can. I know I can fire people without cause and sometime I have. But if I don't have enough employees, customers don't get good service. They may leave or, worse, shoplift. There's only so much I can do myself.

One thing I've learned is when I go away on vacation or to trade conventions–it is better to close the store because my employees will steal me blind. We used to never close but now we have to. We lose money we'd make if we were open but we'd lose more to theft if I'm not there. It's not worth it. That's why a lot of businesses go under. Theft knocks them out. People don't realize this affects everybody.

We still have employee discounts–I even made them more generous–but I don't think it helps stop much employee theft. I have a system to track shrinkage but we're not computerized so it's not as accurate as it could be and we detect it less quickly. I think our younger generation doesn't have the ethics and they have this attitude of entitlement. If they invested half the creative energy they use for stealing to make a better life the right way, they'd go far. It's still sad and frustrating but I'm more resigned to it now.

I've felt hurt and betrayed when employees have stolen from me in the past. Now, I have a slightly thicker skin. If anything's changed in the last two years I'd say I really don't try to get to know my employees–I keep them more at arm's length. This probably isn't good either because then they sense you don't trust them. It makes for a tougher relationship. You try to be as good as you can. I've hired one foreign person who seems to have a better work ethic; she's a church-going woman and I think I can trust her more.

I can't even say family members and friends I've employed haven't stolen from me. A friend of mine just had a shock. They employed a bookkeeper who was like a second daughter to them–they even hosted her wedding at their home. Then they find out she had been embezzling from them for years.

You still have to watch the ones you'd least expect to steal. The better the salesman, the more problems you'll have. If someone is too slick, watch out. It's true. I had a guy who was a real good salesman–too good; it's like "I'll sell one for you but I'll sell two for me."

Notes & Reflections:

Helen's Story (A business owner)

Helen is a dynamic woman in her 50's–a nurse and a small business owner. She is a caring soul, naïve at times and tough as nails at others.

I am the founder of two small, private, non-profit companies, one a research institute and the other a counseling clinic. The companies are 22 and 15 years old. In the beginning, I was very naive. I used to think people who came to work for non-profits believed they were doing God's work or were so committed to serving others that the thought of stealing from the company just wouldn't occur to them. I read in the papers that in for-profit companies, the CEOs and others seem to feel entitled to steal–like at Enron. I felt in non-profit companies, the CEOs and major players would be unlikely to steal because of working for a cause. I was wrong.

In our case–and probably in other non profits–it was our bookkeeper that stole money from us. I think bookkeepers and financial staff may be more likely to steal money from the company. Of course, they have access to the money but they also may not recognize the same calling to serve the greater good as the folks who founded the company or who are directly helping others. Even so, I doubt you'll see a lot of non-profits model Enron–where the motive for stealing is just greed. More likely, you'll find an employee has gotten himself into some type of financial trouble and stealing seems like a solution. I've also read how some people get into trouble for not understanding money and not keeping good financial records and audits.

Time is also something people steal from companies and don't even think about it. They take long lunch hours or go on the Internet and buy property in Arizona on company time. I bet they don't consider that's actually stealing from the company. Maybe they think if they don't have any clients they can just do whatever they want, rather than use their time to catch up on other things or ask fellow co-workers if they need help, or even clean the bathroom if it needs cleaning. I have a strong work ethic–that probably goes without saying as I'm the founder of two companies. Over the years, I've become a little less judgmental about employees who don't work like I do. I know people who work with clients need breaks now and then; maybe the Internet helps–if they just log on for a few minutes.

When it comes to pure dishonesty, however, I just fire employees who steal from the company. I've fired three employees in the last three years. The first was a secretary who was taking money from petty cash. The second one was also a secretary who we knew was a former drug addict. Since we work with addicts, we thought her history would be a benefit to the company. But one of the first signs of trouble was she wasn't getting her work done. She was disorganized. Then petty cash came up missing and then money which clients gave us to hold was missing. Our Vice-President wanted to wait until we caught her red-handed. I said, "Forget that, she's done! She's gone." I just walked her out.

The following week, we got the proof we needed she had been stealing from the company. But she ended up hurting us in the end. It was hard for me to believe she was smart enough to do this–I guess that's my fault. Months before she was fired, she had stolen one of our Director's credit cards, which we used for shopping for office supplies and food. Maybe she took it as an insurance policy in case things got rough and she got fired and needed food for her kids. We thought it was just lost and we called to replace it. We should have just cancelled that card number. Our liability insurance didn't reimburse for any employee theft that occurred more than 90 days after termination. Somehow, she waited just over three months after we fired her and then she went to different stores all over the tri-county area and charged about $800 worth of stuff–just under the $1,000 felony limit. The stores had her on camera but none of the cities were willing to prosecute her. We sent our company attorney to the courts and got a judgment against her but it took a very long time. They never did put her in jail. We lost $800 but it could have been worse. Recently, somehow, we got a little money back–like $75. Apparently, she's paying some of it back.

The third employee fired was the biggest thief of all: "Jimmy" our bookkeeper. He may have been stealing for some time. While we never could actually prove what he was up to, there was enough evidence to file a police report, which we did. He was the star employee. He was nice. He ran the finances for both of our non-profit companies–that was a big mistake. You learn over time.

One of the first clues was way back at his first interview but I wasn't sharp enough to notice back then. One of the questions he asked us during his interview was if we ever kept two separate sets of books. I remember saying to him "two separate sets of books? We can hardly balance one set of books." He probably realized I was completely naive and it would take me years to catch such a sophisticated thief.

For years, I didn't know what was happening. Then, about three years ago, it all came to a head: someone was counterfeiting checks. We hired a fraud team to investigate. We couldn't even use our own financial auditors since this had been happening on their watch. It was so sophisticated. I felt terrible. We struggle to pay our employees a decent wage and here I am–the President–and I allowed someone to take advantage of us like that. I was very angry. I felt cheated.

We had two problems: the first involved sloppy billing and receivables at one of the companies. Our auditor called us in and showed us there were discrepancies. It was difficult to determine, but we suspected he was keeping two sets of books. We began to gather evidence–irregularities such as not writing "For Deposit Only" on the backs of big checks the company received. We noted phone calls from funding sources with questions about his sloppy billing. Further irregularities found by our auditor led us to believe he was stealing, but we couldn't figure out how. My mother was a bookkeeper. She told me he may have been keeping two sets of books. She asked me: "does he carry a briefcase?" I said "yes." Then she asked: "does he need to carry a briefcase?" I said "no, there's no real reason to carry one in and out of our offices." Finally, she asked: "does he bring his lunch?" I said "no, he goes out every day." She said if he isn't using it to bring his lunch to work, he's probably keeping a separate set of books on computer disks in his briefcase.

While investigating billing and receivable irregularities, our bank called and said someone had been cashing counterfeit checks against our other company. I asked the number of the counterfeit check: it was the same number as the next check in our checkbook. The bank faxed over the counterfeit check: it had been signed with my signature stamp. A few years prior, Jimmy asked me to make a stamp of my signature which he could use to sign checks at my approval in advance or when I was out of town. This stamp was used to stamp my signature on the counterfeit checks. The bank said two people were caught trying to cash the counterfeit checks at an out of town bank and had escaped when the checks were questioned by the teller. I then realized the sophistication. I was almost in tears.

We had an internal control procedure in place that required me to open all bank envelopes when our monthly bank statement and cancelled checks came in the mail from the bank. I did this every month. The counterfeit checks were green and yellow and ours were blue. I would have caught that but Jimmy must have been tampering with the bank statement envelopes. He likely intercepted the checks before I opened them since he got the mail. He must have took them to his house and pulled out the green and yellow counterfeit checks. I know Jimmy's wife worked at a bank so he had access to bank envelopes. Then he'd mail the checks back to the company in the new envelopes. When they arrived in the mail, he'd give them to me and everything seemed like it was in order. That could have been happening for years. At our other company, the checks came to a different office and other employees give me the envelopes. Nowadays, I have both statements mailed directly to my home.

We got all the money back from the eight counterfeit checks we found had been cashed. We got it back because late at night, one of my staff and I went to the office and pulled all the computers out of the office. I wanted to prevent him from doing any more damage to our financial records. I also found the signature stamp which was required to be locked up at all times. It was lying next to the printer. Someone had obviously been printing more counterfeit checks and stamping them with my signature.

Jimmy called me at 7:30 the following morning yelling: "You took my computer! You took my computer." So, I knew we'd done the right thing. "Actually," I told him, "it's not really your computer." He knew the game was up. I walked into work with a policeman. He had his things already packed. Some of our staff still haven't forgiven me. They still can't believe he stole from us. Sometimes I can hardly believe it. I actually miss him. I feel like a divorced woman who wants to go back to the good old days before she knew her husband was cheating on her.

The fraud team came in and looked and found he had tickets to Las Vegas; other evidence seemed to indicate he may have had a gambling problem. Who knows? Maybe the two people who were cashing our checks were threatening him. Maybe he owed them money and they were threatening his little son. I remember, just before the end, Jimmy used to say: "Why don't you just fire me?" I'd ask: "What are you talking about? Why would I fire you?" And he'd just say, "I just wish you'd fire me."

Over the years, I have forgiven Jimmy and forgiven myself. I know some staff who are still friendly with him, and that's fine with me. People get themselves into trouble. I heard the secretary who stole our credit card was back using drugs. It's hard to be mad at people who need help. You can have compassion yet not let people harm your company.

When an employee steals from your company, you feel duped, you feel ashamed–duped by the people trusted and ashamed because the others who work for you expect you to be a good steward of company funds. It's a sad, sad thing. You feel really bad and really stupid. Then you just hope it won't happen again. I'm more alert now.

As for lesser theft–like theft of time or theft of office supplies–we don't always terminate for that. A supervisor has to review time cards and they have to be signed in and out every day and left at the front desk for checking.

We're a lot sharper with screening new employees even though we don't have any new test or questionnaire. Maybe we're still a bit naive to assume they're good until they prove differently; if that happens, we terminate them right then. No exceptions. I imagine there are people who think they're entitled to steal if they're upset with me. I think I'm pretty approachable, especially since I'm getting older. There are staff who aren't afraid to take me on. I don't think there are serious morale problems right now at any of our clinic sites.

We also hired a new bookkeeper at each company both of whom are very honest and truly wonderful. We work very closely together. I'm much more involved now which is not my nature or interest. I'd rather be talking to our clients, helping them sort out their issues and move on with their lives. But if you're going to be a small business owner you have to get involved with all the financial affairs to make sure things work and you're not losing money. I've had to step out of my own comfort zone to grow.

Notes & Reflections:

Gary's Story (A store owner)

Gary is an East Coast pharmacist and business owner in his 60's. He's married with two grown children. His wife works with him. He is a charming and soft-spoken man with a good work ethic and a sense of humor.

I've been a pharmacist for 36 years. It's a family business. I wanted to be an engineer. I was going to teach and do research. But I ended up going to pharmacy school and into business with my brother. When I was a teenager, working with my father, I don't remember any talk about theft–there was less of it back then.

When I went into business for myself, I immediately discovered that employees steal. And a lot of them aren't very good at it. They think that you don't realize what they're doing but eventually you catch on. You just seem to know: like with the cash drawer–when it's well under one day or well over another. You get a sixth sense: you know when somebody is stealing–when you ask questions–by their demeanor, the way they're talking or acting. An innocent person answers questions differently from a dishonest person. No doubt about it. An innocent person shows concern, even in the way they talk. I've found–if a person has done something–they don't show concern. They'll say "oh, I don't know how that happened" or they'll go overboard and they'll try to say too much.

Most of the employees I hire now are recommended by other people–either by employees, by customers, or by people I know. Rarely have I put an ad out or a sign out "help wanted." It's mostly somebody who knows somebody. Except if I needed another pharmacist–a more specialized position–then I may need to hire an agency. I've had a group of employees for a long time who help me find new employees as needed. You get to know these people.

However, with that said, I've still been shocked many times by those who have stolen from me. You wonder about people. We had an employee who was stealing phone cards. Another employee was referred to me by her mother who was a dentist's nurse in our building. She turned out to be an out-and-out thief! There'd be $100 missing and I'd ask her about it and she'd say "I don't know." Then a few minutes later I'd count the drawer again and $50 would be missing. I couldn't really accuse her but I made up a story that I no longer needed her help, that a relative was coming back to work for me. It was a funny situation because I knew her mother and I didn't think her mother would believe me anyway–she'd have said "oh, no, my daughter's not a thief."

One thing I found interesting but also disturbing: very rarely do you have an employee tell you about another employee who is stealing even if they know about it–even our loyal employees. I don't know why. After I let someone go, they'll always say "yeah, we knew that was happening." And I'll ask "well, why didn't you tell me?" They always say "I don't know." They just don't want to tell on each other. I guess they don't feel it's their duty. It's disheartening. Perhaps there's a loyalty among fellow employees–they see you in one echelon and they're in another–and they're not there to do your job for you. Maybe that's how they think. Maybe they're stealing, too, so why would they tell on somebody else?–maybe it will come back to them.

We've had problems with employees stealing medications. Back when Viagra first came out on the market, we kept coming up short–no pun intended–on our Viagra. There was one young man who you'd never have thought was the person taking it but I got a call one day from his wife who told me he was taking drugs. A female employee who was still working for us was the one who recommended I hire him. I asked her if she knew he was stealing drugs. She said yeah, I know." And I asked, "Why didn't you tell me?" And there was no answer to that. I had to fire the guy–he was the nicest guy–and he kept begging me he'd never do it again. He even called and called asking for his job back.

There's another case of an employee not telling me about something. I've never thought about having an anonymous tip line or some kind of incentive program for reporting theft. I've been lucky lately; I haven't had anything major happen in a while. I haven't discussed stealing with other business owners except to know that it happens to everybody. One of my friends had to fire his whole staff for stealing.

I've had kids steal from me and adults steal from me, married people with children. They think they're entitled to steal in some sense. They see there's a business with money coming in all the time. They think you're making a lot of money and no matter how good you treat people–they always feel they're entitled to more. They take that little extra, thinking "he won't notice it."

I had a cosmetician–a married woman with a couple of kids, she knew our family–I caught her stealing merchandise, I caught her stealing money. There's only so much you can take. I had to let her go. Typically, I say "I don't need you anymore." They usually put up some kind of protest, some get angry, and some don't. It's always disheartening, it really is, especially when it's someone who's been working for you for a while and you find out they're stealing from you.

The last time I let an employee go–not too long ago–she had an anxiety attack right in the store and I had to call the emergency service to take her to the hospital. She had become so distraught that I let her go. She was stealing–no question about it. She was stealing money and goods and I gave her a couple of chances. I confronted her and she denied it–"no, no, not me, what are you talking about?" One time she owned up to something but she said "so and so did the same thing–she did it so I thought I could, too."

You ask yourself the question: why do they do steal? You try to pay a good salary, you try to give good benefits–I guess it's just not enough for them. I've found that part-time people are more apt to steal than full-time employees. With a few hours here and a few hours there–often with different employers–they have no loyalty. That's something I've learned throughout the years. As a matter of fact, I don't have any part-time employees anymore. But even some of my most loyal full-time employees have stolen from me, too.

I think almost every employee takes something. I really believe that. Whether money or merchandise, 80-90% of my employees–maybe everybody's employees–have taken something over the years. Some of it you may know about and some of it you may not. You put up with it if they're a good employee and it doesn't get to be a major problem. You overlook it or from time to time or you bring it up–like "you know, the register's been a little off, just be more careful with what you're doing" or something like that–if I want to keep the employee. It might stop for a while; if it doesn't or it gets worse, then you just let them go.

It's one of those things where you just can't be there all the time. You try to get people you think you can trust. Then you find out later the trust isn't there. And it hurts, it really hurts. You want to trust these people. I know if I leave for a week it's gonna cost me–no question about it! But when it costs you too much and it goes on all the time–that's when you get rid of the people. It's kind of like a cost of doing business, it's built-in. Just like the shoplifting. You try to keep it down to a minimum. We don't use electronic gates to or security cameras. It's too expensive. We used to have cameras but more as a deterrent–nobody was manning them–but I don't think they worked that well. We've never had greeters or guards–we're a small business. We do have mirrors still but when it gets busy in the store, certain things will come up missing. You can't watch everybody.

With shoplifting, if we really catch them with the

merchandise, we get it back and shoo them out. I've had good customers steal from me–I know they have. I've never confronted them but I watch them. It's been mostly small items. You can't protect everything. We have valuable things right out in the open. You can't sell from locked cases. As you know, you walk into most places today and things are out in baskets, on tables. We have pretty good inventory control but everyone in the store needs to be aware of what's in the store. I'm constantly asking our employees "did somebody steal that or was it bought?"

I try to talk to my employees one-on-one about problems or discrepancies but I've also had staff meetings when something's come to a head. I'll say, "Look, I know there's something going on and I have an idea of who it is and if it doesn't stop someone's gonna get let go." This always helps, in the short term or a little longer. I try to give compliments, raises–I try to be flexible on work times. I try to be as good to my employees as I can afford. But when you find you've been really good to somebody and they still steal from you, it really hits you in the gut. How good can you be? Sometimes I've treated them well to a fault. I feel if I treat them well they should do a good job for me. I've never prosecuted anyone for employee theft. I just don't think it's worth it.

I've had so many people steal from me over the years, it's incredible. Then you get into a good spot and it's great–like right now I have a good bunch of employees. I think the way to protect money, especially, in a small business like mine, is to have family work the cash register. I have my wife at the register and my mother used to work for us. Most people think it's their right to get a little extra. He has so much; I take a little more–maybe that's the attitude. People don't realize how much time, money, and energy it takes to keep a business afloat. They don't stop to think–if the business goes under, what happens to them? Maybe they think there's an endless supply of jobs out there but there's not.

Notes & Reflections:

Sarah's Story (A loss prevention worker)

Sarah, near 40, has been a loss prevention worker for 10 years and has worked at Macy's in a Midwest city for several years. She recently left to work for Old Navy.

I'd say at our current store, 80% of our focus and loss of profit is due to employee theft and 20% is due to shoplifting. Employee mistakes also account for a small percentage of loss. I've heard our stores in different cities have different percentages. In Detroit, I hear there's a lot more shoplifting. I've read some of the book "Something for Nothing: Shoplifting Addiction and Recovery" and I don't know if I agree with some of the so-called common reasons people steal, like anger or loss. There are other reasons.

I'm working everyday on some case of employee theft. Sometimes we catch them right away but more often we have to watch someone over time to build a case. Right now we're investigating an employee who was trying to sneak merchandise out the back door. We check all employees' bags now before they leave work. We have videotapes we use to catch people and we do interviews and interrogations. We have a time limit for how long we can talk to employees–it's not four hours but thirty minutes. We have to try to get them to confess. We have long-time employees who know the system and we have new hires that are naive and try to test the system. Nobody's ever come forward and confessed on his or her own.

We even have housekeeping personnel who think they can shoplift in the store just because the lights are off or turned low. One of them recently put items in a trash bag and then took it out to the dumpster to be picked up later. But our cameras can see in the dark. I had a talk with her the next day. And when I talk to them, I don't just say "we know you did it, you'd better confess." I try to let them know we're investigating and see what they say. Most of the time, they confess. The interesting thing is–9 times out of 10–when I ask them why they stole, they say "I don't know." When they say "I don't know," I give them the benefit of the doubt and start exploring a little more. Within about five minutes, they come up with a thousand and one reasons. I won't have to open up my mouth at that point, they just start talking.

In this recent case, the housekeeper said "My son died." And that was true. Another common reason is "I didn't have any money to buy gifts for my loved ones for Christmas or a holiday." Another thing they say a lot is "everyone in my department is doing it." Then we have the bold ones, the ones who have been working and probably stealing for a long time–they'll say "I'm not getting paid enough and I'm making up for it." When you hear that, you're a bit surprised. Some of them even admit they'd been doing it a long time and thought we knew. I had this one guy say "I thought you knew and it was okay." I try not to laugh sometimes. Some people lie so I have to show them the evidence and the videos but most people come clean about it once confronted.

Now foreign people–employees who have arrived in America more recently–they steal differently. They take their time. They just seem to know in their minds they won't get caught. They feel it's owed to them. They also seem to steal lots of jewelry to give as gifts. They'll tell you the truth. They'll say "I did it because I wanted it and I wanted to give something to my family for letting me work." Or, they'll say "my husband takes my check and I don't have any of my own money to buy something for myself."

We know there's a difference between a professional thief who steals for a living and most of the people we deal with in terms of shoplifting and employee theft. We start with a background check. Our background checks aren't always totally accurate or safe-proof. We ask if they've ever committed a crime other than a traffic offense. A lot of people are going to say "no" and we run a check. Sometimes we do hire people with offenses and keep an eye on them.

We have a great Human Resources Department. We talk about new hires–whether they're being honest and whether they'd make good employees. We won't hire anybody with a theft offense on their record. The only exception is around the end of the year Holiday Season where we hire about 60 people a week; sometimes the background checks don't come back until after someone has been hired. But if we find a theft offense on their record, we fire them. Some of them know their time is limited and leave on their own just as we're getting the background check back.

One person applied to our store after she had been fired for employee theft from our former company which merged with us. We had a record on her and we told her we couldn't hire her. Another applicant was fired from our store in another state and we caught that, too. Sometimes, things slip through the cracks. Our Human Resources Department tries to work with employees who do other kinds of theft like time card fraud. But our philosophy is "if you're doing those kind of things, you're probably doing others, too."

We had a real big case back in October 2004 where a female employee was taking our products and was selling them on e-Bay. We found out by accident when a customer called us instead of the employee–our phone numbers just happened to be similar–and the customer was asking about the products for sale on e-Bay. We did an investigation and put a camera up in the stock room. She was taking things by going out the mall entrance instead of the employee entrance. We put somebody at the mall entrance and let her get out the door and to her car. When we got to her car, she had so much stuff in her car–I can't even tell you. I've never seen it before in my life. She said she was doing it to justify her paycheck. I said "you make a lot of money; you've been here 12 years. Why would you mess it up doing this?" She didn't seem to care. We had to prosecute her.

We have another employee who's been with us for a long time. I know him. I'm surprised but we're investigating him for theft. He's buying things on his credit card and returning without actually bringing back the item—just re-crediting his account so he can keep his balance down. He'll probably say we don't have any proof. He's the one who will probably get a lawyer. We do have some cracks in the system we have to work out. I think he's also bought things, voided them out right afterwards, and kept the items. A lot of employees do that. They also find ways to abuse their employee discounts.

We prosecute everybody. It's time consuming but I think it's more of a deterrent against employee theft. If we just fire someone—as we no longer give references to prospective employers—it's like we pass the buck to the next company who hires someone we fire. We're on the receiving end, too.

We have periodic seminars on loss prevention for our employees. We don't have outside consultants. Every new employee has an orientation and watches a video. I'm always trying to get to know employees and let them get to know me. I think it shows I care about them; hopefully, they'll care about themselves. I'm always giving out rewards—"this person did this, this person did that." I keep a close eye on new employees especially. Recently, we hired a lot of new people and some of them started stealing right away.

My boss has been in Loss Prevention forever. Her philosophy is everybody messes up sooner or later in terms of a work violation—usually theft. The real issue is whether or not somebody keeps messing up. And many do. Another problem is even if people go to jail or to a diversion program—all they're going to learn is how to be a better thief. Every time I come to court, I feel like it's a waste of time. All you hear is why people stole—"times are hard, I didn't have enough money," or "there was a death in the family." We need more "how to live" or "how to survive" classes. Too many people think stealing is worth the risk.

Notes & Reflections:

Hal's Story (A human resources director)

Hal is the Director of Home Office Human Resources for a national restaurant chain. He's in his 40's and is a dedicated and compassionate man. He loves his job and loves people.

I have run the EAP here for the last 17 years. I have a background as a chemical dependency counselor before I came here. I went on for a certification in employee assistance. My undergraduate degree is in business and my graduate degree is in organizational management.

We've taken a global approach to employee theft through our employee assistance program. We believe you can help reduce employee turnover and retain people if you demonstrate, through action, that you care about them and you want to help them if they're having personal issues that affect their work performance.

I wouldn't say we've established a policy that if someone steals from us we are going to rehabilitate them. We certainly don't have that because we have very strict policies about theft at our company. But there are incidences or occasions depending on circumstances where we have offered assistance to employees who have stolen depending on various factors. We take it on a case by case basis. Our policy is if you steal from the company you will be terminated but we leave it up to loss prevention to make the call if they think an employee made a bad decision, if company assets could be recovered, and they felt this person was worth giving help to or assistance to. We'd also help an employee we terminated find help even after termination.

We've seen a lot of employees steal as a result of chemical dependency, gambling addiction, and various financial hardships or crises. We even know absolutely that some people do get addicted to theft behavior itself. And stealing is something all levels of employees engage in–right up to the top. It does not discriminate based on profession. Our Director of Loss prevention and I want to do a study to see how much of our management turnover is due to gambling addiction. What happens to an employee who has general or theft-related issues is based on the needs of that individual.

We have about 65,000 employees; 14,000 are insured. We refer them to counseling whether they're insured or not. We refer them to services with a sliding fee scale, to A.A. or N.A. groups or to government-funded programs. Often, the severity of the offense dictates what level of care they need.

We do have a rough gage when someone has stolen an amount which calls for unequivocal termination but I don't know what that amount is. Bottom line is, if you take a piece of bubble gum from our retail store–that's grounds for termination. But, again, we leave it up to loss prevention– they do their investigation and the employee assistance program partners with them. Then there's a determination of whether to work with the employee and keep them on or whether to terminate them. Sometimes the termination goes bad; we still try to get them help. We realize the consequences of theft can be pretty dramatic.

We don't worry about word getting around our company that we're soft on theft–we're not. I can't tell you exactly how well our employees do who are given a second chance but we have one of the lowest employee turnover rates and one of the highest utilization rates of our employee assistance services–75% seek out help voluntarily, 25% are referred.

Our approach to employee theft is unique. A lot depends on what was stolen, how much was stolen, how honest and cooperative the employee is, and how much we think the employee is worth retaining. We have a working relationship that falls in with the values of the company. We're not soft on theft but we try to look at the whole picture.

Horatio's Story (A loss prevention worker)

Horatio is a loss prevention worker in his 30's. He works for the same national restaurant chain as Hal. He loves his work and prides himself on being an investigator "with a heart"

To be honest, a lot of loss prevention folks today are really just out there to make a case or a make a name for themselves. A lot of them only care what their statistics were last month–and if your statistics weren't good–you're not going to hit your budget, you're not going to get your bonus.

Don't get me wrong–we still prosecute theft in certain cases but we do have a lot of compassion where most companies don't. We give individuals an opportunity to tell us why they stole and, often, we'll be able to work things out. Usually, when a company has evidence against a person for theft, they won't give them an opportunity to talk, they'll just make a police report and prosecute. That's where we're different and, I think, progressive.

Even in cases where we know someone has stolen from us but it's hard to prove, I'll interview the person and tell him what we have. If they don't admit it to me–but they're an otherwise good employee–they stay on because a lot of times just that interview has put enough fear in them because they know that we know. They know we don't have enough proof but they know we're watching them. Those employees tend to leave the company right away or within the year.

Those who have stolen and against whom we do have evidence–who are otherwise good employees–we tend to refer to our Employee Assistance Program. After that, all information is confidential between the employees and that program. I know what happens in terms of whether they stay on or are fired. I know if we find out there are certain reasons why am employee stole, I'll have that person contact our EAP; after that, it's up to them to decide what to do with the employee. We don't have a hard and fast policy of firing people with a drug or gambling habit, but we do tend to be careful about that. The therapists through our EAP are very good. We advertise our EAP to our employees and want them to call when they have problems.

Our company has showed some interest in referring people to C.A.S.A. or for specialized theft-offender counseling but I don't know if they've followed through.

We track all our employees we've investigated through our Sleuth Report software program. We can track the cash registers and things like that. This is how we build a lot of our cases. We've fired people recently who stole without having outside forces contribute to their thefts. We view that as different from people who wouldn't likely steal except for difficulties happening in their lives–who know it's wrong but cross over the line due to some pressure or something.

We have a saying: "it's just a piece of candy." Some employees eat the candy we sell and that's still stealing. We make no bones about that. But if an employee really opens up to us, we don't care as much about how it happened as why it happened–and that's the opposite of most companies' concerns. We'll work forward from there. But if an employee is going to lie to me then I don't have much compassion for that person– to me, they're a bad employee.

Absolutely, we make a distinction between different people who steal based on their reasons for stealing. This has been an approach in this company for a long time. I'm not sure the history behind it. I used to work for another major company that has a very different approach and I'm glad I work for my current company. There's another company which adopts a similar approach; their Director of Loss Prevention and ours are best friends. Maybe we're starting a trend.

Notes & Reflections:

Part Two

New Perspectives

The Bigger Picture

In addition to each individual's own particular life history and personality, we also have to look at the larger stage on which we live and act. I don't think many people would disagree that partly why we are seeing an increase in employee theft is due to shifting economies and decreasing job security for employees and, thus, decreasing loyalty toward employers.

Consider the top stories of any newspaper or radio or TV news program over the last decade:

-more layoffs and more downsizing

-outsourcing of jobs and a shrinking middle class

-cuts in benefits & fewer insured

-corporate CEO's making millions & corporate crime

On top of this, the media is in our face more and more each day implanting images of actors and actresses, singers, dancers, and athletes with perfect bodies, mounds of money, stately mansions, and tons of toys. Many want their share of the pie. Competition, envy, jealousy play their roles, too.

We live in an increasingly materialistic society where money, looks, and possessions determine our value.

It's a changing world. When people get scared, they can go into survival mode–where, often, morality takes a back seat. When people feel the unfairness and injustice of life, they can become angry and disillusioned–the line between right and wrong becomes blurry.

And yet, somehow, no matter what we're going though, we must find a way to do right or to get help to do so.

The Real Reasons People Steal from Work

Hopefully, the previous stories in Part One have already helped you think about employee theft in some new ways. In my first book, "Something for Nothing: Shoplifting Addiction and Recovery," I spoke of the seven types of people who shoplifted. I based this on my research as well as on that of others', particularly the NASP–the National Association for Shoplifting Prevention. The Seven Types are as follows:

1. The Professionals

2. The Drug and Gambling Addicts

3. The Impoverished

4. The Thrill Seekers

5. The Absent-Minded

6. The Kleptomaniacs

7. The Addictive Compulsives

For clarification, by "professionals" I mean–similar to professional shoplifters–there are people in the workforce who are drawing a paycheck but their real intention, often from the get-go, is to gain access to goods or money equal to or in excess of their legitimate compensation. They may work alone or in groups; their primary motivation for theft is greed–it may even become a business in itself.

By "impoverished," I mean to include not just the truly indigent who may barely be getting by though employed, but also those who come into acute or protracted financial stress or crisis due to reasons other than addictions: deaths, illnesses, divorces, loss of jobs, loss of home, etc.

I believe–and research supports–that the great majority of shoplifters fall under the last category; simply, people who steal for reasons other than simple need or greed. Those more articulated reasons are as follows:

1. Grief and Loss, To Fill the Void

2. Anger/Life is Unfair, To Get Back/Make Life Right

3. Depression, To Get a Lift

4. Anxiety, To Comfort

5. Acceptance/Competition, To Fit in

6. Power/Control, To Counteract Feeling Lost/Powerless

7. Boredom/Excitement, To Live on the Edge

8. Shame/Low self-esteem, To Be Good at Something

9. Entitlement/Reward, To Compensate for Over-giving

10. Rebellion/Initiation, To Break into Own Identity

Through my research, my own personal recovery, and my work with clients, I believe these categories and motivations are relatively similar in regards to employee theft.

John Case, CPP, a loss prevention consultant for over 25 years, outlines his seven reasons why people steal in his workbook "Employee Theft: The Profit Killer" (2000). They include:

1. Economic Need

2. Revenge

3. Drug Abuse

4. Boredom/Excitement

5. Lack of Consequences

6. Losses are Undetectable

7. Nobody Cares

In some sense, our lists are similar. But there are some differences.

1. Mr. Case includes gambling as one of the economic factors, assumedly in regard to the debts associated with this growing scourge. I tend to group gambling along with drug addiction as both being similar in that it is the addictive mindset–not just the financial crisis–that largely contributes to the act of theft.

2. Mr. Case speaks of revenge–and I agree anger is a strong factor in much employee theft–but he limits the source of the employee's anger to events or interactions at work. I take this into account while also asserting that many employees "displace" and vent their anger in their personal lives as well through workplace theft. A common example is in an argument with a loved one where the employee feels a lack of power or fairness. The employee gets that feeling of power or fairness back through employee theft. Perhaps working with someone who reminds me of somebody in my personal life with whom I have conflicts brings up conscious or unconscious discomfort.

He seems to weave into revenge the feeling of entitlement as when an employee feels underpaid or underappreciated. I view this as a related but distinct motivation. And, as just stated, employees often "displace" their feelings of entitlement from sacrifices or suffering in their personal lives through workplace theft. A common example of this is someone who is working a full-time job and then having to care for an ill loved one. Feeling over-burdened, one may easily feel entitled to a "reward" by stealing a little extra.

3. Mr. Case places the most emphasis on the problem of drug abuse–casting drug abusers as the primary source of employee theft. "No one who uses drugs can normally afford to do so and the employee is no exception. With over 70% of illegal drug users employed, there is little room for doubt

that 40-80% of internal theft involves substance abuse."

I was a chemical dependency counselor for seven years. While I certainly acknowledge drug addicts make a disproportionate dent in internal losses, their numbers–relatively steady over the last decade–pale in comparison to the overall number of people who steal. Roughly 1 in 10 people are alcoholics and–without minimizing–most are non-violent, do not drive drunk, and do not steal. Drug addicts represent an even smaller percentage of the population; most find it hard to stay employed for very long.

4. Mr. Case speaks of boredom and excitement as follows: "simply put, getting kicks is a psychic need for many people and stealing meets that need." I would say that this may be true for many younger people but I wouldn't underestimate how tragically bored many adults feel with their work; rather than stealing just for kicks, many may be vulnerable to stealing to lift them out of depression or to provide the spark of energy needed just to carry on.

Finally, Mr. Case speaks of three specific beliefs which explain why employees steal from work:

5. Lack of Consequences – "It's a victimless crime."

6. Losses are Undetectable – "Nobody will notice."

7. Nobody Cares – "It's expected; everybody does it."

In my last book, I outlined ten similar beliefs common among most shoplifters. They include:

*"Life is unfair."

*"The world is an unsafe place."

*"Nobody will be there to take care of me."

*"Nobody's really honest."

*"I'm entitled to something extra for my suffering."

*"Nice people finish last."

*"There's not going to be enough money to live."

*"It's a 'dog-eat-dog world' out there."

*"No matter how hard I try, things never work out."

*"It's not worth my speaking up about anything."

But where do these beliefs come from?

I believe we develop beliefs throughout our lives which become our truths. These beliefs fuel employee theft. Most people are unconscious of their thoughts or they may be prone to "stinking thinking." But all behavior–whether freely chosen or stemming from an addictive mind set–originates from our thoughts, beliefs, and values.

Our values come from our families, our peers, our culture– both ethnic and national, our media, and elsewhere. Often, we find ourselves holding conflicting values such as a value toward honesty and hard work and a competing value of finding the loopholes and the shortcuts to the easier job.

Notes & Reflections:

_____

_____

_____

_____

_____

_____

_____

_____

_____

_____

Doing Well, Doing Good, Doing Time

The June 6, 2004 Sunday New York Times Magazine ran an entire series of articles about white collar crime. The cover story was entitled "Doing Well, Doing Good, Doing Time."

One article, in particular, caught my attention: "What the Bagel Man Saw" by Stephen J. Dubner and Steven D. Levitt.

A man named Paul F., a researcher, also delivered bagels to various companies over a span of 20 years. The bagels were left daily at various businesses along with note and a box for each company's employees to pay on a "trust system" for what they ate. Paul F. scientifically compiled his findings.

Paul had expected to see a 95% payment rate based, in part, on his assumption that most people would pay a small amount for a good product and a good service by a man–Paul F.–whom most of the employees had either met or heard of. His payment rate, however, usually fell somewhere between 87% and 90%. In the beginning, "he left behind open baskets for the cash, but too often the money vanished. Then he tried a coffee can with a slot in its plastic lid, which also proved too tempting." He ended up with a wooden box with a slot in it. "The same people who steal more than 10% of his bagels almost never stooped to steal his money box."

"He also believes that employees further up the corporate ladder cheat *more* than those down below. He reached this conclusion in part after delivering for years to one company spread out over three floors–an executive floor on top and to lower floors with sales, service and administrative employees. Maybe, he says, the executives stole out of a sense of entitlement. (Or maybe cheating is how they got to *be* executives.) His biggest surprise? 'I had idly assumed that in places where security clearance was required for and

93

individual to have a job, the employees would be more honest than elsewhere. That hasn't turned out to be true.'"

Paul also "identified two great overriding predictors of a company's honesty: morale and size. Paul F. has noted a strong correlation between high payment rates and an office where people seem to like their boss and their work. (This is one of his intuitive conclusions.) He also gleans a higher payment rate from smaller offices. (This one is firmly supported by the data.) This may seem counterintuitive: in a bigger office, a bigger crowed is bound to convene around the bagel table–providing more witnesses to make sure you drop your money in the box. But in the big office, bagel crime seems to mirror street crime" –in essence, it's not as big a deal or shame.

Paul F. also found, contrary to what he expected, "that as the unemployment rate goes down, dishonesty goes up. My guess is that a low rate of unemployment means that companies (have) to hire a lower class of employee." The data also show that the payment rate does not change when he raises bagel prices, though volume may temporarily fall.

In sum, Paul F. found "that a poorly paying office rarely turns into a well-paying office, or vice-versa. This has led (him) to believe in a sobering sort of equilibrium: honest people are honest, and cheaters will cheat regardless of the circumstance."

Paul may have had that last point almost right. I've heard and read it in several places. John Case reports it in his book as well: 3 out of 10 employees will steal; 4 out of 10 employees won't; and 3 out of 10 will steal if there is opportunity."

Notes & Reflections:

Kleptomania or Theft Addiction?

To be clear, I doubt very many people who commit employee theft are kleptomaniacs. But a kleptomaniac is different from a theft addict. Kleptomania is a relatively rare condition. In his 1997 book <u>Kleptomania</u>, Dr. Marcus Goldman states 6 out of 1000 people suffer from kleptomania. 80% of kleptomaniacs are women, and the average age of onset of the stealing is 20.

Kleptomania is an impulse control disorder. I see most theft behaviors–including employee theft–as more addictive-compulsive disorders.

What is the difference between an impulsive act and an addictive-compulsive act? The answer is timing. Children often engage in impulsive acts–actions without planning or thinking things through at all. Addictions usually begin as spontaneous, curious, or impulsive acts. Then, a pattern develops and the person may entertain some degree of planning or premeditation. Often, a person engages in some weighing of risks or some internal dialogue in an attempt to not steal. Over time, the "addict mindset" gets stronger; many feel utterly compelled to give into their thoughts, feelings, and urges. This is a similar dynamic to alcohol, drug, gambling, and shoplifting addictions.

The classic kleptomaniac steals things when he/she begins to feel anxious. She has discovered, over time, that stealing creates a feeling which counteracts the anxiety. In short, kleptomaniacs steal to reduce anxiety, most people who steal from work steal when feeling angry or entitled.

In addition, kleptomaniacs feel "relief" almost immediately after a theft; whereas, many who steal from work may not feel much relief after a theft until they are out of the office.

Kleptomaniacs typically do not use or need the objects stolen and often discard or hoard them. Kleptomaniacs tend to steal things they can't use, don't fit, or multiple same items–like hundreds of pens. Kleptomaniacs steal for the feeling created by the stealing rather than for the value of the item or the item itself. This is true with many people who commit employee theft. *The taking or accumulation of objects or money creates a sense or power, of getting something for nothing, and tipping the scales of fairness back in balance.*

Some call this simple greed. I think of greed as including a feeling there is never enough *but also* including a disregard for the needs of others which results in trying to keep others from having something–their due–too. That's not most people's concern. Most people aren't trying to keep others from having anything. Most don't even feel like they were really was taking from anybody. Stores and workplaces were nameless, faceless entities; if anything, the common perception of the worker is that the company is the greedy one. *It isn't so much about having more money or stuff as trying to fill a bottomless hole to get back whatever symbolically whatever was taken from me.*

This is not to say that money or objects mean nothing to people. If they didn't, most would discard them right after taking them. *Theft addiction is unique: not only does one get a high from the act of stealing but there's actually something to show for it.* With alcohol, drug, food, and sex addictions, there's only a memory: no physical token or souvenir. Just the act of stealing was what I chased but I enjoyed and benefited from the items I stole–at least momentarily.

Employee theft is most similar to shoplifting and gambling addictions. For these addicts, the money won or the item stolen is the marker of the successful "fix." For the person who steals from work–getting away with it is the "win." But as with gambling, stealing is rarely about the money or the items; it goes right back into the gamble. *It never ends. It's never enough. You keep chasing that rush, that high. You're out of control and don't even know it.*

Comparison between Kleptomania And Addictive-Compulsive Stealing

Kleptomania (DSM IV Rev.)	Addictive-Compulsive Stealing
*Recurrent failure to resist *impulses* to steal objects *not needed* for personal use/monetary value/no premeditation	*Recurrent failure to resist *addictive compulsive* urges to steal objects which *are used*/some premeditation
*Increasing sense of tension *just before* committing the theft	*Generally, *already ever-present tension*
*Pleasure or relief *at the time of theft or during* the theft	*Generally, pleasure or relief *shortly after* committing the theft
*The stealing is *not* committed to express anger of vengeance	*Generally, the stealing *is* a means of acting out anger or to make life fair
*The stealing is not due to Conduct Antisocial Personality Disorder	*Same. Generally, most people are honest and law-abiding

C.A.S.A. Group Demographics & Statistics

My best estimates of some key statistics of the nearly 1000 people who've attended C.A.S.A. in Detroit from 12/92-6/05:

---

*65% women *35% men
*25% age 50–above   25% 40-50   25% 30-40   25% age 30-under
*60% directly court-ordered
*30% begin after arrest but before being court-ordered
*10% "voluntary" (came on own accord)
*60% are primarily for shoplifting
*25% are for a mix of shoplifting and employee theft
*10% are primarily for employee theft
*5%   are for other theft (credit card, from individuals, etc)
*70% have been previously arrested or fired from a job
*25% first arrest or first firing from a job
*5%   never been arrested or fired from a job
*70% report 1st theft as a child
*20% report 1st theft as a teen
*10% report 1st theft as an adult
*25% report stealing nearly daily
*40% report stealing at least 1x/week
*20% report stealing at least 1x/month
*10% report stealing around 1x/year
*5%   report stealing one time
*35% report other addictions (food, alcohol/drugs, gambling)
*75% report shame, depression and anxiety from stealing
*50% report currently seeing a counselor
*75% report have seen a counselor at some time
*35% report taking some form of psychiatric medication
*25% attend CASA over 1 year (stealing virtually stops)
*50% attend CASA for 6 moths -1year (stealing greatly reduced)
*20% attend CASA for less than 6 months (stealing lessens)
*5%   attend CASA one time and never return

Notes & Reflections:

Part Three

New Solutions

Managing the Managers

As the former Director of a counseling clinic with a staff of twenty, I have to admit, I barely had enough time to appreciate what I really needed to feel supported and content in my work, let alone stop and think what my colleagues needed–even though that was my job. I was promoted from within the company and received no real management training. They didn't offer it and I wouldn't have thought I needed it anyway. I was sure pretty sure I was promoted because I wasn't a complainer, I was a quick learner, and I rarely bothered anyone for help. In essence, I was very much like the higher-ups. "How hard can managing be?" I remember thinking. "I'm a smart guy, a hard worker, and gosh darn it, people like me." I was in for a big surprise.

I survived just over two years. I was in over my head from the get-go. I naively thought if I just showed up every day and kept my nose to the grindstone, everyone would just follow my lead. Well, everyone was hard-working all right, but there were complaints, grievances, and downright protests! Maybe things naturally intensify when there's a management change. Maybe they smelled the inherent weakness in my laissez-faire strategy. Or, maybe, it had something to do with my management style–or lack thereof. I recall at each of the three annual employee evaluations, several of my staff evaluated me by saying: "Terry, you don't listen." *Ouch!*

I fell into the trap of desperately wanting to be liked by my staff; I had no training in straddling the delicate balance between engendering respect and being firm while remaining personable and emanating enthusiasm.

I'm not sure how much employee theft was going on at our little company while I was at the helm, but I'm sure if I did a little, others did a little more. As much as I had learned to think like a thief over time and didn't like being taken for a dummy, I really wasn't that attuned to what others were doing in regard to employee theft. I never actually had to fire confront or fire anybody for theft; we periodically discussed issues at weekly staff meetings. On a few occasions, I questioned staff about their time cards.

I had my own frustrations with upper management but didn't realize it until it was too late. I now see how important it is to have good management–because 55% of employee theft is committed by managers and because the morale and behavior of the remaining 45% is heavily influenced by management style. This is likely nothing new to most people but, in the specific context of theft reduction, good management takes on a new importance.

I strongly encourage companies to research and invest in the both the best screening and the best training possible for their managers–the sooner the better.

In the book "Reducing Employee Theft" (1991) by Snyder et al, I found a lot of sound ideas that seem timeless and, yet, progressive:

It starts with investment in the screening process–which "most employers–and managers–view as a necessary evil. Time, more than expense, is the primary issue, and wise managers will take time to address potential problems with employees before the hiring decision is made. First impressions are often wrong–dishonest people can be charming. An ounce of prevention is worth a pound of cure."

Frankly, I don't remember anything ever being said at any

job I'd ever worked–from menial on up–about a company's specific policy on theft. Like many or most, I guess it is either too awkward to discuss or it is just assumed that it is an offense which will result in immediate termination. It seems to me a good idea to discuss a company's policies for termination–if they are indeed clear–up front. Establishing company values and expectations–through a mission statement and other avenues–is vital.

Just as I've tried in my own life to become more assertive and have encouraged my clients to speak up through words rather than–indirectly–through stealing, managers must also learn to be assertive rather than passive or aggressive. Addressing issues of dishonesty must be done promptly and precisely.

Snyder recognizes–as do I–the reality of theft in the workplace:

"Theft is a state of mind–nothing more. Prevention and control are merely states of awareness and caring. Physical security cannot solve the problem because the physical acts do not constitute the problem; the mental attitude behind them does.

"If you treat people like you would want to be treated, then you will be okay. The single most important factor in controlling internal theft is management's attitude toward employees."

It is interesting, however, that in several of the companies I worked for, I truly believe the management felt they were treating the employees well. The management were workaholics who didn't like to hear complaining and that is how they tended to treat the staff. So, something has to shift.

This is where management must foster morale by opening the lines of communication. Snyder describes the "two-way communication" as "giving employees an opportunity to discuss their problems and acknowledging they merit consideration–this provides positive reinforcement for employees and makes them feel more part of the company.

"If an employee is happy, there is less reason to steal from the company and if people feel a part of the company they are less likely to steal from themselves."

So, managers, how do you make people start feeling more part of the company? For some, it's by allowing input and ideas, for others there may be actual ways for employees to become shareholders or have some financial stake in it. Put on your thinking caps, we're on to something here.

Snyder offers another unique approach to help employees feel involved and included: enroll them directly in participating in the development, implementation, and monitoring of solutions to theft problems at work. "Employees will resist efforts geared toward detection but support prevention programs and will more readily accept and act upon conclusions they reach themselves than upon the conclusions of others."

Employees need to understand the effects of losses not only on the company but on themselves personally through less pay, fewer perks, hiring fewer people to help with workload, and–ultimately–in potential loss of job.

We are all connected.

Notes & Reflections:

It's a Family Thing

Like it or not, we are all connected. For better or for worse, we're spending more and more time at the office and working. Statistics increasingly show that many people meet their future spouse at work and many more find primary friendships and social supports through their jobs. We might as well get along. If we can't, then it may be time for a "divorce" and a move to a new work family.

I had a conversation with a prominent businessman whose company has routinely landed in Fortune Magazine's "100 Best Companies to Work For" list. He asked me not to use the interview due to corporate sensitivities around the topic of employee theft but the one thing I feel I can share is the primary notion that his company was founded on the principle that the business is more than a business: it's a family. He, too, believes that theft is lower than the norm because of it.

Now, it's one thing to say you treat your company like a family and it's another to do so. What does treating people like family mean? For many, that idea is a horrifying one. In some cases, families are downright dysfunctional and abusive–who'd want to come to work for that? For others, family implies a kind of closeness or intimacy that may feel inappropriate or violating in the workplace. Of course, there's also the old joke that hiring actual family members is a "lose-lose" proposition: "family members complain when you treat them like family instead of regular employees and they complain when you treat them like regular employees instead of family."

The point is a family–ideally speaking–is a group of people around whom you can feel safe to be yourself, safe to speak your mind, safe to ask for help and safe to make mistakes.

Ideally speaking, a family celebrates you, nurtures you, and supports you in being the best you can be. I believe we all desire that and all need that to function at our best. Ideally, this would have come from our biological family but it often doesn't. That, I believe, is–at its core–why a lot of people really steal. And, so, many of these pains get acted out at work–usually when something at work triggers a memory or familiar dynamic with family.

We're all walking around looking to fit in, to belong, to feel safe. It may sound touchy-feely but–no matter who we are–we're the same at heart.

Increasingly, people are seeking counseling due to work-related issues, stresses, events, and relationships. In my work as a therapist, I often help people understand what core issues (family of origin issues) are being triggered at work. Likewise, issues at home or in the family often spill over into work performance and relationships, and into employee theft behavior.

In my work as a consultant, I feel there is value in offering information about family dynamics and how they mirror work. I offer short and periodic, engaging and interactive presentations with co-workers to demonstrate how family and work relationships are inter-related. Both tears and laughter are common. New awareness is created where there was none before. Co-workers have more empathy for each other when they get to know who they really are. Only in rare occasions would one use vulnerable information about co-worker against him or her. Of course, that is the risk everyone is really afraid of. We talk about this, too. In the end, better communication styles are practiced and better recognition grows of each employee's strengths and challenges. It's like a Meyers-Briggs approach but from a family dynamics point of view. And it works.

The Top Concerns of Employees

Fortune 500 Magazine has published an annual list for years now called "The 100 Best Companies to Work For." It is compiled from actual employee surveys and questionnaires. In looking over some past lists, it appears that employees' concerns have remained relatively consistent. Snyder et al were on to this back in 1991 when they reported a similar survey which was done in 1946. The results were as follows in order of importance:

1. Full appreciation of work done
2. Feeling of being in on things
3. Sympathetic help with personal problems
4. Job security
5. Good wages
6. Interesting work
7. Promotion and growth in the organization
8. Personal loyalty to employees
9. Good working conditions
10. Tactful discipline

By 1986–40 years later–the list remained similar with some shifts in priorities:

1. Interesting work
2. Full appreciation of work done
3. Feeling of being in on things
4. Job security
5. Good wages
6. Promotion and growth in organization
7. Good working conditions

8. Personal loyalty to employees

9. Tactful discipline

10. Sympathetic help with personal problems

Supervisors were also asked which concerns were most important to employees. Interestingly, their answers in the 1946 survey did not change one bit in the 1986 survey whereas the employee's answers had evolved.

As a manager, I was in the dark about my own concerns as an employee let alone my co-workers' concerns. Too often it is easy for managers to get frustrated with what they perceive as constant complaining, loafing, and lack of gratitude. Many business owners and managers are simply amazed employees aren't just grateful to have a job!

The answers from the 1986 list are not substantially different from more recent comments in the 100 Best Companies survey. A few adjustments included a growing value and concern for autonomy, good benefits, manageable work load, and group cohesion.

These lists clearly highlight how important being appreciated is to employees. Instead, we live in a culture obsessed with perfection and criticism and a dearth of praise and appreciation. I have counseled too many people who stole, were depressed or worse–over their anger and hurt in not feeling valued, loved, and appreciated by family. The dynamics of work life are much the same. Job security is a concern–just as marriage security is; and loyalty is a strong group concern among family, friends, or employees.

Again, these theories aren't brand new, but we need to look at them in a new way as it relates to employee theft. We tend to react and oversimplify the issue by judging people as dishonest, greedy, or untrustworthy. Off with their heads– and fire them! Employee theft is like a Medusa which keeps growing new heads.

Tying It All Together

I believe it's vital we know how people who steal from work think. I know many Loss Prevention workers take into account how shoplifters think: that they are more prone to hit stores with poor customer service–including rudeness and long lines–or with tempting product placement. Stores have reduced shoplifting by employing "friendly greeters"–a human presence at the entrance/exit, by offering "freebies" within the store, and by keeping small or expensive items less vulnerable to theft. And what good are the most sophisticated loss prevention systems if the personnel are understaffed, underpaid, and overworked?

Employee theft presents similar challenges and opportunities. It is likely we will play out our family dramas, dysfunctions, and authority issues in the workplace. The stresses of the job itself–or stresses in our personal lives–are rarely dealt with effectively by even the most progressive human resources departments. On the issue of employee well-being, many employers simply take the stand: "that's not our job."

For every high profile case of employee rage and violence, there are many quieter acts of anger–employee theft.

Why not try something new? We don't have to throw everything out but, rather, add some things that might actually work. The workplace is like a second home and, far too often, we are breathing in toxic fumes without even knowing it. A workplace is like an aquarium. We are like different breeds of fish that need to get along together.

What if regular periodic meetings were held–facilitated by a neutral, outside, skilled consultant–to air grievances, offer apologies, and express compliments and gratitude to "keep the tank clean"? What if confidential counseling were available for those who knew they had a theft problem?

I hope I have shown in some new way how real people become vulnerable to stealing from work. Most don't want to do it. Most don't like who they become once they start. I hope we can wake up and make adjustments in the workplace which can deter some degree of theft. Some people, naturally, are going to need more help. I believe it's possible to send a strong message that theft is not okay while also being proactive and offering help to those who could benefit.

As with drug, alcohol, and gambling addictions, we must first recognize that a problem exists. Some jobs will put up with all kinds of behaviors associated with addictions which cost a company money: absenteeism, negligence, low productivity, sexual harassment, and minor dishonesty. But, somehow, theft is seen in a different light. This may be party, but not fully, justified.

Employee theft is in our midst already, despite whatever strong messages there are against it. Why not try something new? Specialized counseling and groups have worked for other addictions. Someone has to take the first step.

Even if terminating an employee is inevitably best for the company–and, often, the employee–aftercare referrals and facilitated exit interviews or meetings may prove valuable. I once facilitated a reconciliation session between a business owner and the employee he fired for stealing from him. Both got to express what they needed to express and they are now friends again. No, he didn't rehire her–that's not the point. They both learned from their mistakes and took a bad situation and–rather than look at it solely in black and white terms–gained something valuable from it.

I hope we can see employee theft as not just a challenge but an opportunity for us all.

Notes & Reflections:

Part Four

Exercises for Recovering Theft Addicts

Questions for Self-Exploration

1. Recall your earliest memory of stealing something that didn't belong to you. What did you take?

2. What was going on in your life at the time that may have been significant?

3. What did you think and feel about your action?

4. Was there anything symbolic about what you stole?

5. Were there any negative or positive consequences from your action?

6. Did you develop a habit of stealing things soon afterwards or later? If so, how long was it?

7. When you were a child, did you witness someone else steal or engage in dishonesty? What was the stolen?

8. What was going on in your life at the time that may have been significant?

9. What did you think and feel about this other person's action(s)?

10. Are you aware of any negative or positive consequences for that person or for you because of that person's action(s)?

11. Did you develop a habit of stealing things soon afterwards or later? If so, how long was it?

12. When you were a child, do you recall any incidents of things having been stolen from you literally or symbolically? What was stolen?

13. Did you know who stole this from you? If so, who?

14. What was going on in your life at this time that was significant?

15. What did you think and feel about having something stolen from you?

16. What did you think and feel about yourself?

17. What did you think and feel about the person(s) who stole from you?

18. Are there particular kinds of things that you steal? What are they and why do you steal these kinds of things?

19. Are there particular jobs you've stolen from? Where and why?

20. Have you noticed that you began to steal more things, larger things, more expensive things, more money, or more frequently over time?

21. Are you more prone to stealing at a particular time of the day, week, and year? If so, when and why is that?

22. Are you more prone to stealing when you are in a certain mood? Anxious? Angry? Lonely? Depressed? Manic?

23. Are you more prone to stealing when a certain event or circumstance occurs? If so, explain.

24. Do you actually use or derive benefit what you stole? Explain.

25. Are you able to distinguish between your desire for what you've stolen and your need for it? If so, explain.

26. Do you experience strong feelings or physical sensations right before, during, or right after you've stolen? If so, describe the sensations and when they occur.

27. Do you tend to be perfectionist and need control or order? If so, do you think this is a factor in why you steal?

28. Do you recognize any other addictive or compulsive behaviors in your life? What are they and how do they relate to your stealing?

29. Who knows about your stealing and to what extent?

30. What prevents you from telling certain persons or from elaborating to the ones you have told?

31. List all the benefits, financial and emotional, that you have gotten out of stealing? Be honest with yourself.

32. List all the financial, emotional, legal, and employment-related that stealing has cost you. Be honest with yourself.

33. Do you want to stop stealing? Why and why not?

34. What are you prepared to do to support yourself in stopping and not starting again?

35. What have you learned about yourself from these questions?

My List of Unfair Things

Acknowledge that you feel like a victim and feel it as fully as you need to. But also acknowledge that you cannot change the past and you cannot control the future. Acknowledge that, in some way, this is may be what you have been attempting to do through employee theft–undo or make-up for the past and buffer future pain and disappointment. And you got hooked. We got hooked. Where do we go from here?

What if we surrendered the notion of fairness altogether? What if we learned to live life on life's terms and accept that sometimes things go well, sometimes better than we thought, and sometimes they don't go as we wish? For "recovering victims" like me, I know what it feels like to feel like life rarely or never goes my way, like I'm not getting my reward, like I am being cursed or punished. It is a very painful way to live but, at least, I get to be right about it and have plenty of evidence to support this.

There are still too many days when I'd rather be right than be happy. So much of the world falls into this trap. When do we really get to enjoy life? Can we ever just attune to a place of wonder, surrender, letting go and living in the moment? And if so, why doesn't it seem to last? We need to be careful about dwelling on my feelings of self-pity and my thoughts about life being unfair. Making a list of unfair things helps us put in out there in a concrete way to take a look at it. *The goal is not to dwell in the list but to name it feel it, and release it.* You may wish to burn or bury the list afterward.

Think of all those things you hate about your life or feel are unfair. Really run with it! Don't hold back or edit yourself out of guilt. We've all been told not to complain or whine. Let it rip! Your intention is to get it out so you can let it go. What's the worst that can happen? You'll either end up in tears of sadness or tears of laughter, or both!

Your List of Unfair Things (Go for it!)

1.

2.

3.

4.

5.

6.

7.

8.

9.

10.

11.

12.

13.

14.

15.

16.

17.

18.

19.

20.

My Lucky Gratitude List

No matter how bad you feel your life has been, there is another side of the coin. You are still alive. You may not view that as a good thing. But recovery requires us to begin thinking in a new way. When someone comes to C.A.S.A. devastated from a recent arrest or job termination, certain their life is over–that the judge is going to lock them up forever, their family is going to disown them, they'll never work again–it reminds me of the power of thought. In my 13 years of hearing these stories, the worst has never happened. That's not to say people didn't lose things–they did–but most of the time things turned out much better. Many come to be grateful for their bottoming out: it steered them toward help and toward a greater appreciation of basic gifts: freedom, family, friends, health, comforts, and opportunities.

We made a list of unfair things because we needed to bring that out to see what keeps us from feeling grateful, lucky. I'm a classic worrier and I lean toward pessimism easily. It's like the old joke: "What's the difference between a pessimist and an optimist? An optimist thinks this is the best of all possible worlds. A pessimist knows that it is." Or another way of saying it: "An optimist's creed is, gratefully, 'It doesn't get any better than this.' A pessimist's creed is, ungratefully, 'It doesn't get any better than this.'"

Is the glass half-full or half-empty is a trick question. Why even look at the glass like that? If there's water in it, be thankful there's water in it. If it's empty, why not be grateful there's a glass there to catch the water from wherever it comes? We get to choose which list to focus on.

Think about any lucky breaks you've had in life. Think of things that could have been worse but they're not. It's time to put your thinking cap on. If you are having trouble, ask someone close to you to prod you in the right direction.

Your Lucky/Gratitude List: (Just Do It!)

1.

2.

3.

4.

5.

6.

7.

8.

9.

10.

11.

12.

13.

14.

15.

16.

17.

18.

19.

20.

My Dream Job

Write a description of your dream job if money didn't matter, if age didn't matter. Really go for it! Was it something you dreamt about as a kid? What excites you about it?

_____

_____

_____

_____

_____

_____

_____

_____

_____

What has kept you from going for it? Is stealing somehow an attempt to make up for the pain of not living your dream job or career? Is it working? What steps can you take to move closer to your dream job, even on a part-time basis? Can you taste some of the dream even as a hobby?

_____

_____

_____

_____

_____

_____

_____

_____

If It Were My Business

Write some thoughts and feelings to the following questions:

If you had a store or business, how do you think it would feel to have employees steal from you? What would you do in response to this? What would you do—in terms of security, policy, and "corporate culture" to reduce or prevent theft?

_____

_____

_____

_____

_____

_____

_____

_____

_____

_____

_____

_____

_____

_____

_____

_____

_____

_____

_____

_____

_____

_____

_____

Journaling

Journaling is an important tool–especially for recovering persons. Journaling may include diary-like writings, poems, doodles or drawings, recording of dreams, and checklists. Journaling is a great way to voice or vent whatever you're going through. It also helps you look back more objectively and clearly and recognize important patterns over time.

Journal Example

Things were going well at work until the end of the day when I was coming up the stairs and I overheard a conversation by two female co-workers who were complaining about me, belittling me. It was like a spear harpooned through my heart. I stopped in my tracks and wondered what to do. Part of me wanted to slink back down the stairs without them knowing. Part of me wanted to run up and tell them to "Fuck off!" But the hurt and wounded part of me wanted them to know how much I was hurt. So I walked up the stairs slowly until I stood in front of them. They could tell I heard them. They were silent. I told them softly but sternly "I heard that." I went into my office and didn't know what to do.

In the old days, I probably would have taken something like some stamps or office supplies; or, I might have lied on my time card. Instead, went back downstairs, got in my car, and drove around. I pulled over after a few minutes and started banging on the steering wheel, yelling every swear word in the book. Then I started to cry. After a good five minutes, my whole body seemed to drop. I took the rest of the day off, went to the gym to work out, and took a hot tub and sauna. I called my buddy Lee up on the phone and vented.

Another way to journal is, more simply, writing short sentences to help you identify feelings. Five primary feelings are happy, sad, mad, afraid, and guilt/shame.

I feel angry when you don't appreciate me.

I feel hurt when you bring up the past

I feel sad when you don't pay attention to me

I feel afraid when we have trouble paying the bills on time

I feel happy when we have quality time and don't criticize

Practice Journal Page

_____

_____

_____

_____

_____

_____

_____

_____

_____

_____

_____

_____

_____

_____

_____

_____

_____

_____

Gray Area Dishonest Behaviors

Every recovering person becomes acquainted with gray area behaviors. Gray area behaviors may seem like "lesser" forms of the primary addiction but still compromise one's recovery and constitute relapses. For example, a recovering alcoholic whose primary drink was hard liquor might rationalize drinking beer, though it's obvious to others it's basically the same thing. The alcoholic may have agreed drinking beer was not acceptable but as his life became more manageable, he decided he could imbibe a little. He rationalized a sip of champagne at an occasional celebration was okay.

Gray area behaviors keep the denial system alive and likely contribute to full blown relapse. Here are other examples:

*The gambling addict no longer goes to the casinos but still bets on sports or buys lottery tickets.

*The drug addict no longer uses heroin but still takes Tylenol with codeine.

*The compulsive overeater switches from junk food to more nutritious food but still compulsively overeats.

*The sex addict stops seeing prostitutes, having affairs, using pornography, but becomes hooked on Internet interludes.

Each person draws his or her own "line in the sand" about what recovery means and how much addictive behavior to eliminate. Ongoing counseling and/or support groups explore and challenge these gray area behaviors. As denial breaks, deeper levels of understanding develop, and behaviors naturally change for the better.

I report my gray area behaviors openly and honestly at C.A.S.A. each week. Others have shared theirs as well. We have frank discussions about whether this or that is stealing, whether it constitutes a relapse, and how to avoid repeating the behaviors. Recovery is about progress not perfection. It is an ongoing journey. But we never condone gray area behaviors; rather, we emphasize the costs: guilt and anxiety, loss of faith, full relapse, humiliation, rejection when caught. We believe that stealing in any form is a sign of holding onto anger and fear, a refusal to let go and trust life, others, and ourselves.

What rules do you bend? And what's the breaking point?

Your List of Gray Area Behaviors

List all your gray area dishonest behaviors. Be honest with yourself if with nobody else. Write down your rationalizations for engaging in these behaviors. Write down your perceived benefits from engaging in these behaviors. Then write down the negative costs or potential consequences of each.

Gray Area Behavior

I. Using office supplies for personal use

Rationalizations

1. It is not stealing

2. Everybody does it

3. The company can afford it

4. I am using these at work

5. I do other things for free for my company

6. It is a small perk

7. Property should be shared

8. As long as it's only a little, it's okay

9. I deserve a little reward or something extra

10. I don't have time to go to buy them myself

Perceived Benefits

1. I get a good feeling of getting a little something extra

2. It saves me time on going to the store, my time is valuable

3. It keeps me from taking bigger things at the office

4. It keeps me from stealing elsewhere

5. I avoid conflict because I am getting something back

6. It helps me put up with the low pay–I reward myself

7. It comforts me to know I have this to help me

8. It helps me look forward to coming to work

Costs/Consequences

1. Keeps me looking over my shoulder, afraid of getting caught

2. Could be embarrassing if I am discovered

3. Could be fired if I am found out

4. Feel ashamed, secretive, loss of good eye contact

5. Compromises my recovery

6. Feel hypocritical

7. Deprives me of the chance to directly feel feelings, deal with issues, and live life on life's terms

8. Deprives me of practice being assertive at work as it becomes easier to keep quiet, unnoticed

Your List of Gray Area Behaviors

1.

2.

3.

4.

5.

6.

7.

8.

9.

10.

Healthy/Legal Ways to Get Freebies & Good Deals

We all love a bargain. We all love to get something for nothing. Be creative and come up with some safe, fun, natural alternatives to fill that need *occasionally:*

Examples:

1. Coupons

2. Flea Markets/Thrift Stores

3. Only buy sale items

4. Go to free sample days

5. Create art or functional items through creativity

6. Festivals, art/health fairs often offer free stuff

7. Garage sales

8. Estate sales

9. Volunteer for experiment studies

10. Auctions

Others:

-

-

Caution:

I mention these alternatives as legal, enjoyable substitutes for getting "something for nothing." But each person's recovery is different. For some, these alternatives may not be appropriate. People with addictive personalities, by nature, tend not to be able to easily moderate and balance.

I've met a few people who have "coupon addiction." They obsess about gathering coupons, saving coupons, using coupons, altering coupons, hoarding coupons. This is real and can interfere with your life. You can end up spending more money with coupons when you over do it and buy things you don't really need. This may lead to shame and agitation which may trigger urges to steal.

I credit Terence Gorski for following work on Triggers, Warning Signs and the exercise "How My Addiction Served Me." I also thank Personalized Nursing LIGHT House, Inc., for having employed me as a counselor to teach this material to many clients over several years.

Common Triggers & Ways to Cope

Triggers are stimuli I encounter in my external environment, namely, people, places, things, or events–that can set off a chain reaction of thoughts and feelings leading to a relapse with stealing. Recovery includes avoiding triggers that put me at risk and developing coping skills to deal with them if/when I need to. This will require lifestyle changes.

Some examples of triggers and coping skills may include:

I. People

1. My Boss, co-workers (qualities may include: critical, non-appreciative, authority figures, lazy, gossipy)

Coping skills:

1. Avoid, limit contact or length of time around

2. Have a heart to heart with him about how I feel

3. Journal about my feelings

4. Talk about issues in C.A.S.A. or other support groups

5. Work on issues in therapy

6. Talk to family/friends about my feelings

7. Use self-talk/affirmations while visiting

8. Do deep breathing as feelings come up & leave

9. Write him an e-mail or letter stating how I feel

10. Assert my boundaries and behaviors I won't tolerate

II. Places

1. The Workplace (obviously) or work-related venues

Coping skills:

1. Avoid or limit trips to stores

2. Develop new places to spend time (gym, movies, museums, and your own home)

3. Create a buddy system with someone positive at work who you look forward to spending time with

4. Decorate your office space in a soothing, affirming way

5. Take entitled breaks and lunches

6. Go outside for some fresh air

7. Keep smooth rock in your pocket as a reminder

8. Get involved so you feel more invested in your work

9. Join a health club to keep me out of stores (I won't have as much money left over for shopping anyway)

10. Play soothing music

III. Things

1. Office supplies, time cards, cash, checks, the telephone, company credit cards, food, the computer

Coping skills:

1. Avoid contact with if possible

2. If encountered and feeling agitated, do breathing and self-talk and leave

3. Aversion therapy with therapist or self if strong

4. Ask someone at work to remove objects

5. Remind self that possessing the object will not bring happiness

6. Journal about my feelings/experience

7. Talk about it at my support group

8. Find other things to do to take my mind off it

9. Give self a new, better kind of treat or reward

10. Yell or exercise to burn off any tension created

IV. Events

1. Information or changes including the following: poor performance evaluations, failure to get a raise, a cut in benefits, getting fired or laid-off; even non-work related events like someone close dies or becomes ill, a romantic break up; even positive change–like a promotion–can create stress, feelings of loss of control, and fear. Anniversary dates or holidays are also events.

Coping skills:

1. Increase my awareness that an event could bring up strong emotions and potential relapse

2. Make an appointment to discuss issues with a therapist

3. Talk to boss, supervisor, or EAP about your concerns

4. Make sure I am not alone for long

5. Journal my feelings

6. Pray and meditate

7. Attend a support group

8. Don't isolate, hang out with good friends

9. Work out at health club, take sauna, hot tub

10. See psychiatrist for medication if need be

Common Warning Signs & Ways to Cope

Warning signs are stimuli in my internal environment (thoughts, feelings) as well as behavior patterns (lying, for example) which are like red flags. If unchecked, they build-up and will contribute to a relapse of stealing.

I. Thoughts

1. "Life is unfair," "I'm not appreciated," "work is no fun"

Coping skills:

1. Notice the negative thought pattern and don't give in to it
2. Counter this thought with a new thought such as "Thank you for sharing" or "Yes, life feels unfair right now but stealing doesn't really help"
3. Begin deep breathing
4. Slow down, lay down or meditate on a new thought, your breath, or your body
5. Journal the thoughts and feelings
6. Talk to someone
7. Engage in primal scream or go for a walk to release stress
8. Pray to see things differently
9. Review or make a new gratitude list
10. Do volunteer work to help those less fortunate

II. Feelings

1. Anger, Anxiety, Disappointment, Frustration, Boredom

Coping skills:

1. Notice the feeling pattern, don't judge it, don't give into it

2. Begin deep breathing

3. Allow yourself to feel the feeling fully

4. Allow yourself to release feeling cleanly and harmlessly

5. Engage in primal scream or anger release like breaking a stick or hitting a pillow

6. Talk to a therapist, friend, or co-worker

7. Exercise

8. Journal feelings

9. Take yourself out to lunch

10. Do positive self-talk

III. Behaviors

1. Isolating, beginning to engage in "gray area" dishonesty, becoming passive and stuffing anger instead of asserting myself, judging others, stopping going to meetings, care taking others

<u>Coping skills:</u>

1. Notice the behavioral pattern, acknowledge its danger

2. Begin deep breathing

3. Ask yourself why you are doing this; are you really committed to your recovery?

4. Speak with a therapist, friend, or sponsor

5. Journal about it

6. Go to a movie

7. Create something artistic

8. Go for a long walk

9. Start moving your body and let sound come out

10. clean, organize, do a project

List your top 10 triggers & coping skills:

Triggers   Coping Skills

1.

2.

3.

4.

5.

6.

7.

8.

9.

10.

List your top 10 warning signs & coping skills:

Warning Signs   Coping Skills

1.

2.

3.

4.

5.

6.

7.

8.

9.

10.

How My Addiction Served Me

Be honest. You know you were getting something out of your addiction. Despite the negative consequences, despite the attempts to stop and the powerlessness to do so, all addictions serve the addict. There is a payoff, a perceived benefit. It is crucial to get clear on this not only to increase your self-knowledge but to better implement ways to meet the needs you were trying to fill by stealing.

A key to recovery is developing new ways to cope with issues, new ways to get needs met. This takes patience and discipline because we get used to trying to get quick fixes to needs and develop robotic and automatic ways of doing this.

For Example:

I. *I stole to calm myself when I was angry*

*Payoff: It protected me from my anger because I was afraid to feel it or release it on others

*Cost: By using stealing as a way to suppress/avoid my anger, I now realize it continued to build like a pressure cooker. I was still angry and always on edge

*New way to serve need. I can work on my anger and my rage from past unresolved issues as well as when anger comes up in the present in therapy, in support groups; I can journal or exercise.

II. *I stole to fill the void of loss*

*Payoff: It helped distract me from the pain of the loss. It made me feel full for a while, complete. It numbed the pain. It filled the hole. It numbed the sadness, the anger

*Cost: By stealing to fill the void of many losses in my life I realize I didn't allow myself to go through the necessary grieving process we all have to go through. Through stealing, I lost much more.

*New way to serve need: I can attend support groups or counseling, create meaningful rituals (going to grave side, lighting a candle, talking about the good times).

III. *I stole to feel power, to feel control*

*Payoff: I could get something back–at least it seemed–by stealing. It made me feel special and powerful. If I didn't have enough money or enough influence in my life, stealing made me feel less vulnerable.

*Cost: I had an illusion of power and control but, eventually, the tables turned and I felt more disempowered and out of control. It became clear to me that my very inability to stop stealing was a sign I had become a slave to it.

*New way to serve need: I will follow through with positive goals in my life and chart my success. I will remind myself that true power comes from with–from my strength of character–and from without–through my Higher Power. I will associate with people who help empower me and remind me of my strengths when I am down.

Exercise: Complete the following payoffs, costs, and new ways to serve your needs for the following ways you identify stealing served you.

IV. I stole to lift my self-esteem when I felt inadequate

*<u>Payoff</u>:

*<u>Cost</u>:

*<u>New way to serve need</u>

V. I stole to give myself a lift when I felt depressed

*<u>Payoff</u>:

*<u>Cost</u>:

*<u>New way to serve need</u>:

VI. I stole to occupy myself when I was lonely

*<u>Payoff</u>:

*<u>Cost</u>:

*<u>New way to serve need</u>:

VII. *I stole to make life right when life seemed unfair*

*Payoff:

*Cost:

*New way to serve need:

VIII. *I stole to give myself something when I felt frustrated always giving to others, it was a way to reward myself*

*Payoff:

*Cost:

*New way to serve need:

IX. *I stole when I was afraid to ask for help or be assertive*

*Payoff:

*Cost:

*New way to serve need:

X. *I stole because it made me feel smarter, cleverer*

*<u>Payoff:</u>

*<u>Cost:</u>

*<u>New way to serve need:</u>

Others?

Honesty Is Its Own Reward

"Honesty is its own reward" is an old saying and I was brought up believing this. Then something went awry. If honesty was so great, how come there were lies and secrets? Nice, honest guys didn't always finish first. At some point most of us learn not to be so naive and rigid about every rule of life. But giving up on honesty is a dangerous decision.

Once, while Director of a chemical dependency clinic, a young client brought me a check in an envelope that our company had written to a local business. He claimed he found it on the ground and expected to be acknowledged for his honesty–financially. He was truly amazed when I just gave him a heartfelt thank you and a smile. He couldn't believe it. He felt this was a breakthrough for him–actually returning a check instead of trying to cash it as he apparently had done before. I admit, he was so persuasive I was tempted to give him a reward out of guilt. But, instead, I told him to sit with just the acknowledgment of his honest behavior. He went away. The next day he came back to the office for his counseling treatment and told me he had gotten the lesson. By this time, the staff had discussed this event and decided to give him a gift of some sort to show our appreciation for his growth. He was pleasantly surprised when, after letting go of his feelings that we had been unfair, he got a reward on top of his own reward for being honest.

Honesty promotes:

*Trust
*Self-esteem
*Being given responsibilities
*Good relationships
*Admiration and respect
*Spiritual connectedness, serenity
*Others being honest with you

Losing Your Edge or Gaining Your Edge?

It sometimes pained me to think that if I stopped stealing I'd "lose my edge." I still had a belief that good guys are boring and don't win in life. To throw in the towel–to stop stealing–was to give-up my "edge," my ability to tread the line of fearlessness.

I've come to realize the real edge is learning how to be myself. The real edge is having nowhere to run to when feeling angry, depressed or anxious. The real edge is surrendering control over my need for control, over my manipulating life from moment to moment–learning how to be where I need to be. I still find that hard at times. I still fall into the familiar trap of expecting things to go my way if I am good, if I do the right thing, if I am honest. Sometimes they do, but not always. There are no guarantees.

I have an edge in recovery that is much more real than when I was stealing. My edge is more in full view now; it used to be more "behind the scenes" or in a biting joke or remark. My edge is in my ability to be present.

Still, I've had to grieve the loss of "slickness" I honed during my days of stealing. I could probably get away with stealing for a while again, but I know I'd be much more nervous, clumsy, and more likely to get caught. I don't dwell on this, though. I'm actually grateful. Have you ever heard the saying "he's too smart for his own good"? That was me. My slickness–taking short cuts–only got me into trouble in the end. Recovery reminds me I have chosen a different path.

As I bring my new edge into the workplace, I may feel uncomfortable and others may have to adjust to the new me, the real me. But it will be worth it. There's no greater feeling than coming to the office at ease enough to be oneself.

Be Assertive!

I am convinced many people steal from work as a substitute for not asking for what they really want. Most of us have been trained not to be selfish, to put our needs last. We are not taught how to speak up for what we want and need. We are not taught to be assertive. We either remain passive, become violent or aggressive at times, or--more frequently-- act out passive-aggressively through stealing. We take out our anger or other feelings at the workplace: that's indirect and doesn't deal with the source. I'd say one of the top three topics at C.A.S.A. meetings is how to be more assertive in our relationships--with spouses, family, children, friends, the boss, co-workers, everybody. There are many good books on how to be more assertive. Find one that works for you.

Have you asserted yourself lately? With whom and on what issue do you need to be assertive? When will you do it?

WHO?	WHAT ISSUE?	WHEN?

1.

2.

3.

4.

5.

The Importance of Humor

Having a sense of humor about my life and life in general has been one of my biggest challenges. Most addicts have a great sense of humor yet are incredibly sensitive and often take too much in, let too much affect them. We take on the world's pain at an early age; we either care too much or care too little. This must change: a healthy balance must arise. There's hardly a place more in need of humor than at work.

Given the pain and injustice many of us feel, the hardest thing is to laugh at ourselves. How do we do that? First, we need to rule out whether clinical depression or a chemical imbalance is contributing to our doldrums; consider seeing a psychiatrist. Second, we may be blocking energy by holding onto the past and/or fearing the future; consider seeing a therapist or joining a support group. Third, we may need to look at our current environment–family, friends, co-workers; maybe we need to be around people who know how to have healthy fun; consider joining a club, taking up a hobby, or learning stand-up comedy. Seriously! Fourth, diet and lifestyle may also affect our mood, energy, and outlook.

Laughter and joy live in the present moment. If you've ever caught yourself in a good belly laugh, you'll recall that you let go of your attachment to the past and to future. You were in the moment. True comedy is an art and a gift. It gives us back the gift of the present.

So what's so funny about being addicted to stealing? Not much if you are in the throes of it. But can you at least see the absurdity of believing your peace and salvation comes from money or things and stealing them? It is sad to admit but true. You are not alone. Have you ever thought someone else's behaviors were ridiculous or childish? It's time to turn the mirror on ourselves! *The truth will set us free. But first it might piss us off.*

Many have used humor as a defense mechanism or cover-up to protect themselves from pain. We may receive benefits through humor unless our pain can no longer remain concealed. "Fake it till you make it" is a popular saying. This can work for a while.

I remain a recovering "serious person." For those of us who grew up early and took on being reliable, responsible and self-sacrificing, the anger and pain takes a while to melt and give way to lightness, spontaneity and joy. Others before us have been able to realize this. What do you think prevents us from experiencing this? It is most likely our own ego and stubbornness. This is recovery: letting go of the belief that life is unfair, cruel, unsafe, and empty.

"Let go and let God" is a favorite saying in recovery circles. But what does it mean? And how do you do it? When things aren't working out the way I'd like them to, I have choices: I can get angry or upset, I can keep trying, I can do both, or I can give up and quit.

Today I can laugh at myself, even at my painful times and my addictive thinking and behavior. It doesn't mean I don't feel the pain of it but I am grateful for what my addiction experience has taught me. I am glad I took my lemons from life and made lemonade.

I love to tell jokes and most people know me as a jokester. The people closest to me, however, see the other side: the overly serious side. One of my little known passions is to be a stand-up comedian. I finally took a class in late 2004. At the end of the class, I performed with my classmates on stage. It was great! I also write funny songs on guitar and sing them at parties whenever I can. Reading funny books and watching funny TV shows or movies helps me laugh, too.

How do you find humor? What makes you laugh?

Someone to Talk To

All addictions thrive on shame and secrecy. It's imperative you find at least one trustworthy person you can share your story with. People in your life already know or have some idea you have stolen. *We're only as sick as our secrets.*

However, telling another person about your secretive behavior should be done with the intention to get support to help stop the behavior. I don't recommend confessing to alleviate your guilt and shame just enough to continue stealing. For the one listening, it's not your job to fix or save the person who has been stealing. But by accepting no real commitment from him or her to get help to stop the behavior, you may inadvertently send a message you are condoning it.

What might be most helpful is to tell a loved one who has been stealing: "I'm glad you have shared this secret with me. I appreciate your trust in me. You are not a bad person but this behavior is destructive to you, to others (and to us). I need you to commit to getting help for this immediately because our relationship cannot be healthy as long as you are doing this and I can't be in a relationship like this."

Recovery is an ongoing and deepening commitment to changing behavior patterns which, in turn, change you. Stopping stealing is a process which, over time, results in a stronger ability to choose and commit to life. Each day I must make a choice not to steal. Some days this is not a big deal; on others, it is extremely hard to resist returning to the old ways of trying to cope with feelings and life.

But the bottom line is this: stealing does not help me. Stealing doesn't solve anything and never will. "Once is too many times and a thousand times is never enough."

What To Do With The Stolen Money or Items

For many members in C.A.S.A. and clients I've worked with, this issue has resurfaced time and again: What do I do with the things or money I stole? For most, this may be a difficult decision. *There's something primal about possession.*

Relinquishing our attachment to what we stole is valuable and powerful. It is part of a making of amends. Holding onto stolen goods or money, in my opinion, is a form of not letting go, a form of holding onto the past. I advocate getting rid of, or returning, the "tainted fruit of the bounty." But timing is the key. There's a line between letting go too abruptly and dragging your feet.

When you feel ready to let go of the stolen goods, I suggest you do so a little at a time, throwing them away, donating them, or safely returning them to work. One can return an item anonymously through the mail or leave it at a doorstep. Send a short note and some cash. It would be great to take everything back directly to the work, apologize, and arrange some other restitution. This, however, can be dangerous and risky. You may open yourself up for termination and prosecution which may not be the best thing for your recovery and may continue your stealing due to trauma. If you have a therapist, you may wish to explore whether the items you stole had any particular symbolic value for you.

If it's money you've stolen and you have the funds to repay it or make restitution, think about doing so. You may wish to do this anonymously or have some proof of payment if legal issues are possible. If you don't have the money, you may need to find a way to pay a little at a time or explore alternative ways of making amends in a way that works for you in your heart or through negotiation with the company or employer you stole from.

151

The Dangers of Transferring Addictions

Addicts tend to stop one addiction and return to an old addiction, develop a new addiction, or cross over the line to an addiction "in progress." An example is someone who stops smoking and then develops or re-activates a food addiction. When an alcoholic gives up booze, he or she often substitutes caffeine. Many addicts latch onto dysfunctional, co-dependent relationships in early recovery.

Here are a few common addictions which recovering theft addicts tend to pick up as they let go of stealing:

Gambling Addiction

People who steal from work must be gamblers at heart. I never considered this at first because I've always hated gambling in other forms–casinos, card and sports betting– because I've valued balance, stability, and hard work. But I must admit, there's a part of me that needs to live on the edge. *Stealing is a form of gambling.* Each time we stole from work we were gambling that we'd get away with it. We were gambling with our money, our job, our freedom, our reputation, our future because if we were fired or prosecuted, all that might be taken away. Stealing is like Russian roulette to me now. Fortunately, I choose not to play.

Gambling addiction can get activated in a heartbeat when one stops stealing. We're still going to be looking for that rush, that high. Even an innocent trip to a casino can get us– whether we win or lose. I don't go to the casinos. They attract addicts like moths drawn to the flame and are no place for a recovering person to be anyway.

If you feel the need to gamble or seek thrills, take up a hobby like skydiving, rock climbing or something that challenges your mind, excites you. Let the excitement of personal growth work engage you. Give it time.

Shopping Addiction/Shoplifting Addiction

A lot of people who steal from work are already shopping addicts. There was an episode on Dr. Phil in May 2005 which highlighted this. Our society promotes shopping addiction, materialism and consumerism. How does one define shopping addiction? Some have referred to it as "compulsive buying."

Dr. Donald W. Black, in an article on the subject, defines it as *"chronic, repetitive purchasing that becomes very difficult to stop and ultimately results in harmful consequences."* Such consequences can be unmanageable debts, fights with spouse or family members over expenditures, neglecting other financial, physical or emotional needs by spending money elsewhere, and avoiding issues or feelings by shopping. If a person starts out with a shopping addiction, it becomes tempting to start stealing from work to save money or spend money one would otherwise use to shop.

Shoplifting addiction, as outlined in my first book and as mentioned in many of the stories in Part One of this book, is also epidemic and very similar to employee theft: it becomes easy to rationalize and is highly addictive. It is also very shameful and may be easy to hide from others for long periods of time. Little specialized help is available.

Overeating

With all the publicity of late about rising obesity rates, overeating has become one of the quickest, easiest, and, often, least expensive ways to reward ourselves. Studies show that many people tend to "emotionally eat" when they

153

are experiencing strong or uncomfortable emotions. People literally eat their fear and anger to keep it down. Don't do it. I've seen too many clients turn to food as a quick reward. See a nutritionist or, at least, find a food plan (not a diet!) which is healthy, realistic, and balanced. Ask for help and be open to others who may show concern.

What other addictions do you have to watch out for?

Forgiving Ourselves

It's hard forgiving others who we have harmed us. It's hard forgiving life, God, the world, for not living up to our hopes and expectations. Forgiving ourselves, however, may be the hardest journey of all.

I'm tremendously self-critical. The tape is always there, playing in my head. It's been hard to forgive myself for things I did in the past. I'm no longer holding onto any guilt or shame over hurting the stores any of the people in my life. It's more about forgiving myself for being human, making mistakes.

"Shame" stands for:

SHOULD

HAVE

ALREADY

MASTERED

EVERYTHING

I forgive myself for _____

I forgive myself for _____

I forgive myself for _____

I forgive myself for _____

I forgive myself for _____

I forgive myself for stealing.

I forgive myself. I forgive myself. I forgive myself.

What do you need to forgive yourself for?

The 12 Steps to Recovery from Theft Addictions

The 12 Steps have been adapted from Alcoholics Anonymous, which was founded in 1935. They can be used effectively with virtually any addiction-recovery self-help or support group. Prior to starting C.A.S.A. in 1992 I was vaguely familiar with the 12 Steps, particularly the Step 1 notion of having to admit powerlessness over something before being ready to change.

My first support group experience was over a two year period (1991-92) when I attended S.O.S. (Secular Organization for Sobriety). This was not a 12 Step group. When I started C.A.S.A. in 1992, I adopted the looser, more familiar model I'd learned from S.O.S. Some cross-talk may be allowed and there was no Higher Power focus. Some members clearly embrace spirituality as an integral part of their recovery. C.A.S.A. touches on issues the 12 Steps outline but more loosely. We have a phone support list but no formal sponsor system.

Over the years I have learned more about the 12 Steps. I studied them in social work school, worked with them in my own life, and taught them–to the best of my ability–as an addictions counselor since 1997. I feel different approaches to recovery exist. I look at the 12 Steps as a valuable tool. For anybody already working the Steps with any addiction, they can just as easily be applied to recovery from theft addictions. For those unfamiliar with the Steps, I encourage you to study them, read literature about them, and attend a 12 Step meeting. If you decide to start a group for theft addictions, the 12 Step approach has a good track record and provides some immediate structure right away.

The Twelve Steps of Alcoholics Anonymous

1. We admitted we were powerless over alcohol — that our lives had become unmanageable.

2. Came to believe that a Power greater than ourselves could restore us to sanity.

3. Made a decision to turn our will and our lives over to the care of God as we understood Him.

4. Made a searching and fearless moral inventory of ourselves.

5. Admitted to God, to ourselves and to another human being the exact nature of our wrongs.

6. Were entirely ready to have God remove all these defects of character.

7. Humbly asked Him to remove our shortcomings.

8. Made a list of all persons we had harmed, and became willing to make amends to them all.

9. Made direct amends to such people wherever possible, except when to do so would injure them or others.

10. Continued to take personal inventory and when we were wrong promptly admitted it.

11. Sought through prayer and meditation to improve our conscious contact with God, as we understood Him, praying only for knowledge of His will for us and the power to carry that out.

12. Having had a spiritual awakening as the result of these steps, we tried to carry this message to alcoholics, and to practice these principles in all our affairs.

The Twelve Steps of Alcohols Anonymous have been reprinted with the permission of Alcoholics Anonymous World Services, Inc ("AAWS"). Permission to reprint and adapt the Twelve Steps does not mean that Alcoholics Anonymous is affiliated with this program. A.A. is a program of recovery for alcoholism only—use of A.A.'s Steps or an adapted version of its Steps in conjunction with programs and activities which are patterned after A.A., but which address other problems, or use in any other non-A.A. context, does not imply otherwise.

The following are some thoughts to help guide in using the 12 Steps to recover from addictive-compulsive stealing.

Step One

Admitted we were powerless over our stealing–that our lives have become unmanageable.

It took me a long time to admit this and even now, like any addict, it is easy for me to slip into the belief that I am cured and have it whipped. "Denial is not just a river in Egypt" is a popular saying in recovery circles. For a while I told myself my stealing was a choice–after all, I didn't steal everyday (not in the beginning at least) and there were periods of time where I was able to stop. This is very common. I stopped for months after an arrest or confrontation or after starting a new phase of my life, like school or a relationship.

Ultimately, however, I still was powerless over stealing because I always felt the need to come back to it. Powerlessness may be measured by "not getting the lesson." By 1990, after two arrests, several job losses, and a broken relationship, I still couldn't stop. Stealing had become my drug. No fear of any consequences could deter me.

I was also in denial for a long time that my life had become unmanageable. I knew things weren't always going to go my way–in terms of money, grades, romance, emotionally, or clarity of purpose–but I didn't realize how unmanageable things became. I stole as a way of managing my feelings, my circumstances, my conflicts, my relationships.

Maybe you haven't hit your bottom yet. It's not a matter of if…. but, rather, when. For many of us, there always seems to be a lower bottom to hit before we wake up.

WAKE UP!

It's time to admit stealing has taken over our lives! It has taken over! Our lives have ˙become unmanageable and stealing–when we look at it, hasn't really helped. It's hurt us and it's hurt others. It has been a life of lies, of smoke and mirrors. If stealing were the solution, why are we still depressed, anxious, unhappy, unfulfilled? What problems have multiplied?–legal, financial, work, health, self-esteem, relationships, spiritual? For many of us, it was all of the above. But there is hope.

Powerless is how we felt at the start and we tried to get our power back through stealing. But that didn't work. We felt even more powerless over our lives and, eventually, over our stealing. We need to repeatedly come back to the sanity of a Step 1.

Step Two

Came to believe that a Power greater than ourselves could restore us to sanity.

Step One and Step Two came together pretty closely for me. When I hit my bottom in early 1990, I f reached out for help by entering therapy–that was a Power greater than myself.

It is often said in recovery circles: do not make another person your Higher Power. For a short time I needed to. My therapist was my Higher Power. I had prayed to God to take away my urge to steal and that hadn't worked for me. I chose to believe God put therapists on earth to assist as well.

In my asking for help I must have had an inherent belief that I could also be restored to sanity; if I'd ever known sanity. I wasn't too sure about that. But I knew my life had become insane and would just get worse without help. Since then, I've been on the road to ever-increasing sanity... with a few detours along the way. I view sanity as a continuum. Many people don't know how to define sanity, much less experience it.

What does sanity mean to you? For me it means thinking and behaving in a way that really works. It means neither running from nor being overwhelmed by feelings. It means living not in the past or the future, but in the present as much as possible. It is a state of inner peace and knowing that no matter what happens everything will work out.

Employee theft is an outward insane expression of our inner insanity and angry, fearful, twisted thinking. For a long time, I viewed life as insane and rationalized that stealing was the only sane thing for me in an insane world. Many of us believe our addictions are a logical and sane response to life.

In time, we become more spiritual and can access a Higher Power. To do this, we stop or slow down and breathe. We ask ourselves the right questions and allow ourselves to be guided by the Higher Power and wisdom within ourselves.

Step Three

Made a decision to turn our will and our lives over to the care of our Higher Power as we understood this.

It's one thing to admit we've got a problem and that our lives have become a wreck; it's another to admit that we need help and, in a moment of faith, believe that something better is possible for us. But it's a quantum leap to turn our will over, the way we've always known.

Even today, I feel Step Three is the hardest step for me. I see how it's so easy to go in and out of taking my will back. For me, Step Three means not only resisting my will or desire to take shortcuts in life by stealing but actually surrendering my attachment to how I think life should go. After all, this was what really prompted my stealing to begin with: feeling life was unfair and I was, somehow, entitled to make up for it.

Almost every day I am faced with that issue head on. Some days are easier than others but I'm still working on it and always will.

When faced with the temptation to steal, the "lower power" in us would have us believe there is no other way to ease the pain—we are entitled to steal and not to steal is actually a defeat rather than a victory. My own will is the part of me that speaks first and speaks loudest. When asked what I want, this part of me says: "I want that thing. I want to hurt someone. I want to get even. I deserve this!" My Higher will responds, when I surrender, to what I *really* want: peace, love, cooperation, to know everything will be okay.

Step Three asks us to turn our lives over to the care of our Higher Power. Sure, I've said "I've trusted before and look what happened? My way may not be the best way but if it doesn't turn out, at least I can blame myself."

Step Three is a leap of faith. It's no wonder most of us, especially addicts, have trouble letting go of our own way and being open another. When I have done this for moments at a time, things usually turn out better than if I had tried to manipulate or handle it myself. For example: My stealing was an effort to make life fair, to get one up on life, but as much as I tried to do this I kept feeling one down. It was insanity, like a mouse going back to the cheese which is no longer there, doing the same thing over and over again and expecting a different result. I could have kept fighting but gradually I realized there had to be another way. I had to let go of my way of going it alone and expecting things to improve. I wouldn't have been able to complete this book if I kept trying to do it myself. My Higher Power guided me to the help of others and to surrendering my battle against life.

Step Four

Made a searching and fearless moral inventory of ourselves.

Step Four has been challenging because it called me to stop blaming the world and look at myself. That was hard to do at first and remains hard when I fall back into feeling like a victim. I began Step Four with my therapist in 1990 when I had to look within–not only at my theft behaviors–at all the my less honorable behaviors. I had to own my shadow side, the things that I didn't want to claim, the aspects of myself I projected onto others, especially onto my father.

In working Step Four I also needed to *recover* the positive aspects of myself–the moral parts of myself–which, due to my shame, I had lost touch with. I believe that's where the word "recovery" comes from. I had to recover those parts of me: the truly caring, honest, pure parts. In some ways, it was harder for me to acknowledge the positive aspects of myself than to acknowledge the negative ones.

Step Five

Admitted to our Higher Power, to ourselves, and to at least one other human being, the exact nature of our wrongs.

I confided in my therapist some general details about my stealing but not really the exact nature of my wrongs. I only discussed my shoplifting but not my employee theft. I hadn't been specific about what I had stolen, how much and from whom. It was not enough merely to admit I had stolen. Some slight catharsis came with that but nothing lasting.

Further, the exact nature of my wrongs include not only the surface behavior–stealing–but my wrongful thinking underneath: my selfishness, my greed, my controlling, my impatience, my pettiness, and my resentments. To simplify, I acted mostly out of fear rather than love. I chose fear rather than love and trust. And I had to forgive myself for this. I did the best I could at the time.

Step Five asks we admit this to three sources: Higher Power, ourselves, and another human being. There's the old saying, if we can't be honest with anybody else, at least be honest with ourselves. But sometimes it seems hard to be honest with ourselves unless we make the effort to share with someone else. Somehow, only after sharing with another, do we remember and realize things we've either forgotten or repressed. I've found the same thing to be true when opening a dialogue of prayer, confession, or forgiveness with my Higher Power–whether in my mind, out loud, at a place of worship, at my father's grave, writing in a journal. There are many ways to do this. Each will find his or her own way.

In a sense, I've told the world about my stealing by writing this (and my previous) book and through interviews in magazines, newspapers, on the radio and TV. We must be mindful who we choose to tell–it's a risk because we can't know for sure how one will react. But a good start is to pick an impartial, nonjudgmental person such as a minister, rabbi, therapist, sponsor, or trusted friend–or maybe at a confidential support group meeting.

Step Six

Were entirely ready to have our Higher Power remove our defects of character.

Step Six is like Step Three for me. Being entirely ready to do anything is scary for most; to open for real and accept deep change can feel like facing death, surrendering to death, leaping off a cliff into the great abyss.

What is meant by defects of character? This is tricky. I see these as any parts of myself which lead me or others to suffer. This can be impatience, perfectionism, greed, dishonesty, selfishness, etc. Step Six–as with all the steps– is not likely to be mastered but, rather, constantly practiced. It is meant to be repeated over and over again. So don't feel afraid "you have to get it right" the first time–that's our perfectionism. We move into Step Six when we have worked through the first five. Enter with a spirit of sincerity and purity in the moment. Meditate on it and open to the inner wisdom and power of it. Be curious. We don't need our character defect list in front of us–we likely know what they are; they don't make us bad people but they keep us from experiencing deeper serenity and growth. Just be open.

Step Seven

Humbly asked our Higher Power to remove our shortcomings.

Shortcomings and character defects are related. A character defect may be my impatience. My shortcoming may be my impatience with my wife when she takes more time to do something than I would. My perfectionism may be a character defect. My shortcoming may be how I criticize someone when they don't do something up to my standards.

I'd also like to emphasize the word "humbly" because it reminds us we can't do it ourselves. We don't make demands on our Higher Power; we ask and we are patient. Addict put our faith outside ourselves–in quick fixes–whether that faith is in drugs, gambling, or stealing. Recovery wisdom recognizes each Step is an ongoing process. We may need to ask many times for our shortcomings to be removed as we become more and more ready. Over time, we will gain increasing clarity what our shortcomings are.

Step Eight

Made a list of all persons we have harmed and became willing to make amends to all.

Through my recovery, I saw I hurt many through my stealing–not just as a direct result of what I stole, but also as a result of the lies, the betrayal of trust, and my inability to love others more fully or to let their love in. My secret, addictive life deprived them of the person they thought they were in relationship with.

On my list of those I harmed are the jobs (and people) from whom I stole–some I've known personally, others I have not. I spent time imagining the harm I did to them. It's hard for most theft addicts to feel this because the workplace may feel impersonal and we may not see directly the damage our stealing causes. It's easy to slip back into feeling like we, ourselves, have been the real victims both in life and in our work. Nevertheless, make a list of any individuals, companies, and loved ones, you've stolen from–both tangibly and intangibly.

Step Nine

Made direct amends wherever possible except when to do so would injure people.

Making direct amends is another ongoing process. Amends may begin with an apology but usually requires more. I always say: *The best amend we can give to our friends, family and society is our developing a good recovery program and ceasing to engage in destructive behavior.* To make amends for lost trust takes time and patience; respecting people and property each day is a great way to start. I started a support group for, in part, as a way to give back to society for what I had stolen.

As for restitution of money and/or goods stolen, this may also be necessary. But we need to ask: can confessing or making restitution do more harm than good to others–including you? Ask: what is my intention? Is it just to make myself feel better or is it really to serve others? Sometimes, we'd like to give back what we've stolen but we don't feel we can risk it. Maybe an employer (former or current) won't forgive us; maybe they'll fire or prosecute me–which can hurt me and my loved ones. Would anonymous restitution be appropriate? These are issues to discuss with a therapist, minister, or sponsor.

Step Ten

Continue to take personal inventory and when we are wrong promptly admit it.

This step is very important. Recovery is a process of unraveling and letting go of the past. In the meantime, however, we are living in the present, creating new conflict (or karma) each day, each moment. If we clean up after ourselves as we go along, we create less of a past mess to clean up later. Keep it simple. One of the biggest gifts I've gotten out of my recovery is the ease to admit when I'm wrong. Saying "I was wrong," "you're right," or "I'm sorry," are some of the most liberating words you can speak. A good time to take a personal inventory is at the end of the day or in a support group setting.

Step Eleven

Sought through prayer and meditation to improve our

conscious contact with our Higher Power as we understood this, praying only for knowledge of our Higher Power's will for us and the power to carry out that will

Some people ask "why pray or meditate? I'm not stealing anymore, my life is manageable again." I've been there; often, I'm still there. It's a question of what works and how to realize the full value of recovery. Addicts are good at fooling ourselves into thinking we have control again—we were the sole cause of the problem and the sole solution. This may seem like an empowering belief. It is not. It is dangerous. I know I played a major role in how I got addicted to stealing but I am also a product of my genetics, my family, my environment, my culture, my world. I need help beyond myself to be myself. Einstein said, "the problems of the world cannot be solved at the level of thinking when the problems were created."

While recovery may help me think more clearly, left to my own devices without checks, accountability, and support, I will likely return to my old thinking. Been there, done that. Prayer and mediation also help. There are many forms of prayer and meditation. For me, each is a way of helping me feel connected to the whole, of centering me, of bringing forth my most authentic and powerful self. Without meditation, I've found again and again, my ego runs rampant and, even if I'm not stealing, I remain miserable and tense. The promise of recovery holds much more than this.

Step Twelve

Having had a spiritual awakening as a result of these steps, we will try to carry this message to other addicts and practice these principles in all our affairs.

In a way, I leaped right to Step Twelve by starting C.A.S.A.

before I'd even worked through the other Steps in any thorough way. But I also needed the group to help me realize the Steps. Step Twelve is not an end but a beginning. It is the logical turnaround before returning to Step One. "We only keep what we give away" is a common recovery saying. If I truly have achieved some level of spiritual awakening through my recovery, why would I want to keep it to myself? I'm not saying, go out on the street corner, start preaching and recruiting. But we can carry recovery as a gift to share with others who may show up in our lives–whether at a meeting table as a newcomer or in our daily affairs. As a recovering caretaker, it's very tempting to try to save others again when I am the primary one I need to save. There's a balance. We shall find that balance one day, each day, readjusting from moment to moment. One day at a time.

The Serenity Prayer

God,

Grant me the serenity to accept the things I cannot change,

The courage to change the things I can,

And the wisdom to know the difference. (Just for today)

Notes & Reflections on the 12 Steps:

Part Five

Related Issues

Probation /Counseling/EAP Assessment for Appropriate Referrals to C.A.S.A/Therapy

Note: *These are preliminary assessment questions to help guide you. Use all helpful means of gathering information.*

Questions:	Appropriate	Not Appropriate
1. Are you remorseful over having stolen?	"Yes"	"No"
2. Previous record or firings from stealing?	"Yes"	"No"
3.Have you suffered a recent loss in life?	"Yes"	"No"
4. Are you depressed?	"Yes"	"No"
5.Are you angry/upset about anything?	"Yes"	"No"
6.Do you feel guilty/ ashamed of stealing?	"Yes"	"No"
7. Do you steal from places besides work?	"Yes"	"No"
8. Do others know you steal?	"No"	"Yes"

Totals: _____ / _____

Questions:	Appropriate	Not Appropriate
9. Do you sell any of the items you steal?	"No"	"Yes"
10. Have you tried to stop stealing but been unable to?	"Yes"	"No"
11. Do you know why you steal?	"No/Yes"	"Greed/Need"
12. Do you want to stop? If so, why?	"Yes"	"No"
13. Do you steal to sell things to get drugs, alcohol or for gambling?	"No"	"Yes"
14. Do you steal due to lack of money?	"No"	"Yes"
15. Do you steal alone?	"Yes"	"No"

Totals: _____ / _____

Note: *If the interviewee has identified with most of the questions in the "Appropriate" column, he/she is a good candidate for C.A.S.A. and/or therapy. If he/she has identified more with the questions in the "Inappropriate" column, consider AA/NA/GA, or other forms of correction first. Some persons are not appropriate for C.A.S.A. or therapy. NOTE: Explore all answers more in depth.*

Other Helpful Questions

1. Why did you commit this act? (Explore grief, anger, anxiety)

2. When is the first time you stole something?

3. What was going on in your life at the time?

4. How long have you been stealing from work?

5. Do you commit any other acts of dishonesty?

6. Are you currently in counseling or on medication?

7. Have you previously been in counseling or on medication?

8. Are you under financial stress?

9. Do you have other addictions (alcohol, drugs, gambling)?

10. Do you feel you steal due to emotional stress?

11. Do you feel you are addicted to stealing?

12. Would you consider seeing a counselor and/or attending a local support group for people who steal?

13. Does anybody else know about your stealing?

14. Do you feel guilty or ashamed of your stealing?

15. Have you tried to stop before?

Getting Fired/Prosecuted:

What You Need to Know

Most people's first firing is a shock to the system. Most I've worked with have felt like victims most of their lives and tend to focus on their perceived, or actual, mistreatment by their boss or company–not to mention the police, the judge, probation officers, even their own attorneys. Often, getting fired and/or prosecuted further stokes a person's underlying feelings of anger and unfairness. Where does the cycle end?

Subsequent terminations, prosecutions and court dates elicit fear of being punished more severely for the repeated offense. I've heard countless stories about the anxiety of feeling "like my life is in limbo" while waiting for the final outcome. This may last months to years.

I highly recommend consulting a good employment attorney if you have legitimate questions about an employment issue, especially a termination. Sometimes, employment attorneys may handle a criminal defense matter as well; if not, I recommend consulting with a good criminal defense attorney. In addition, if there are medical, psychiatric, or psychological issues relevant why you committed employee theft, good letters from treatment providers may prove helpful in legal proceedings.

For those who have never been arrested and for those who have gone through legal proceedings but it felt like a blur, the following steps usually apply in criminal offense procedures:

1. Waiting. Waiting to be formally charged after your arrest (notice usually comes by mail or phone from a police detective). This can take a week to several months as the police show the evidence to the local prosecutor who makes the decision whether there's enough evidence to prosecute.

2. *Preliminary Exam.* There is the preliminary exam on a felony charge or an arraignment on a misdemeanor charge. A felony is an offense punishable by more than one year in jail or prison; a misdemeanor is punishable up to one year. With most employee theft offenses, one usually can be charged as a felon if the value of the items or money stolen exceeds $1,000.00 (One Thousand Dollars). A misdemeanor charge is anything under $1,000.00.

In the preliminary exam, initial witnesses are called (store security, police officer, etc.) order to testify about the details of the offense and the arrest in for a judge to determine if there is reasonable suspicion the crime was committed by the defendant. It is not a full trial and guilt beyond a reasonable doubt need not be shown.

The defendant's attorney can waive the preliminary exam or let it be held and cross-examine witnesses. In cases where witnesses fail to show or the judge determines the testimony and evidence against the defendant is nil, the charge may be dismissed after the preliminary exam. If the exam is waived or held and the judge finds there is reasonable suspicion the case is "bound over" to the circuit court for an arraignment.

3. *Arraignment.* In the circuit court for felonies and in the district court for misdemeanors, this is the stage of the case at which the formal charge may be read and an initial plea of guilty, not guilty, stand mute, or no contest is entered. It is also the stage at which to request a court-appointed attorney or have some time to hire one. If a guilty plea is entered at this stage, there may be immediate sentencing or, more, likely, referral to the probation department for a "pre-sentence investigation" or "interview" (PSI) prior to returning before the judge for sentencing.

4. Pre-Trial. The pre-trial conference is the plea bargain or motion filing stage. It usually takes place one to two months after the arraignment if a not guilty plea is entered. A guilty plea can be entered on this pretrial date and immediate sentencing or referral to probation for a PSI occurs.

5. Trial. The trial date (before a judge or a jury) is usually a month or two after the pre-trial. A guilty plea usually may also be entered on this date.

6. Sentencing. The sentencing date before a judge occurs after a guilty plea or a conviction at trial; sometimes there is immediate sentencing after the plea or conviction–usually with first-time offenders; more often, a PSI is requested. The PSI may be scheduled that day or within a month. Formal sentencing usually happens within a month after the PSI.

7. Probation. Instead of–or in addition to–being incarcerated, most people who are convicted are put on probation. This is a time period, usually six months to two years, and may be reporting or non-reporting to a probation officer. It can include fines and costs, community service, attendance in counseling, education groups, support groups, or other court-ordered programs, or the wearing of an electronic tether. If you violate any term of probation (new arrest, unpaid fines, no-show for appointment, etc.) you will likely extend your probation period, add additional costs or duties, or go to jail.

8. Expungement. Misdemeanors–and sometimes felonies–can be removed from your criminal record after some years have passed–usually five–without further incident. However, law enforcement may always retain some back-up record of its having been there.

9. Restitution. Repayment of money or value of goods or return of goods may be necessary in exchange for no prosecution or as part of a criminal proceeding plea bargain or sentencing. Often, it may be hard to gage an exact amount owed. Periodic payment plans are likely if the amount is substantial. If a former employee doesn't keep to the agreed payment plan, prosecution is an option. There usually is no statute of limitations–an employer can press charges almost indefinitely. If one fails to make payments after prosecution, jail could result. Consult your attorney if you are having trouble making payments.

10. References/New Job Applications. Increasingly, most former employers are reluctant to divulge any employment information or give references–good or bad–to prospective employers. This has primarily occurred over the last decade due to lawsuits against employers who may have subjectively or inaccurately given information which hindered one's employment opportunities. Now, as a matter of policy, most companies just don't do it.

This is unfortunate as employment history is one of the strongest indicators of character and future performance. Companies don't have valuable screening information. In addition, an employee who knows about this is less likely to be deterred from stealing as negative consequences are limited. Companies simply "pass the buck"–the terminated employee–to the next company.

If you are a person terminated for theft, you may still have some explaining to do if your work history is sporadic and has gaps or shorter employment stints. Technically, you still need to be honest about whether you quit or were fired; a prospective employer can at least make a call to confirm that even if not the details. Very few companies will hire a liar.

If you have been prosecuted and there is a conviction on your record for theft (or any other offense), it is recommended you tell the truth. The wording of the questions often vary: some ask if you've ever been convicted of a felony, some include misdemeanors, and some even ask if a conviction was "in the last five years." Background checks may or may not be done. Many think it is a chance worth taking: "I might as well lie because they won't hire me if I tell the truth." Many have been hired and fired afterward.

It would be nice if we lived in a world where we could tell the truth. For those who had a theft problem but got help for it, some employers would appreciate the honesty and–at least–put the employee on watch or probation. Many more, however, would refuse to let "a fox in the hen house."

Conducting an Intervention

Since my last book, interventions have garnered more widespread attention. In early 2005, The Arts & Entertainment Cable TV Channel (A & E) began airing an hour-long Sunday night series called "Intervention." The program follows the lives of real people near the bottom of their various addictions and, unbeknownst to them, culminates in actual interventions with family, friends, and a trained interventionist.

I've worked with family members and friends of addicts who've struggled with whether, how, or when to confront or intervene with a loved one. For family or friends of people who steal from work, this is especially challenging because of the shame and misunderstanding about these behaviors and the few resources to direct them to for help. It's tempting to shout: "Hey, you're just a thief! Cut it out! Don't you know it's wrong?" This approach, or similar ones, will only push the person farther away from opening up, getting help, and stopping the behavior.

I've talked to parents of children who steal and to many adults whose parents attempted to address their stealing. *Two approaches don't work:* saying or doing nothing, which sends an unspoken message it is not a big deal; and shaming, yelling, condemning, which sends the indirect message "you are bad" and pushes a child into shutting down his or her feelings. Children steal for various reasons–to get attention, to get a need met, or to test the bounds of their own power and authority. It's really much the same thing with adults.

Most people are unaware, at least for a long period of time, that a loved one has a problem with employee theft. The person stealing usually hides this and even clues like getting fired from work may be downplayed by lies or false explanations. The "evidence" often is circumstantial and you may hesitate to accuse someone. After all, what if you are wrong? Until you find some obvious clue(s), you may feel awkward about whether, how, or when to broach the subject. There's a difference between a confrontation and an intervention. Confronting is typically in the early stages; intervention usually is necessary after the problem has been brought to the light but nothing seems to be improving. Sometimes, though, intervention is the first step.

If you are reading this book, you hopefully have some knowledge and sensitivity about the dynamics and reasons people steal from work. Remember, it's often an unconscious cry for help. It's easy to be mad at someone but he or she is in pain. You also have the advantage of pointing a person who needs help in the right direction: to this book, to our web site, to counseling, to support groups or the various resources listed at the back of this book.

As Vernon Johnson, author of <u>Intervention</u>, defines it:

"Intervention is a process by which the harmful, progressive, and destructive effects of (an addiction) are interrupted and the (addict) is helped to stop (the addiction) and to develop new and healthier ways of coping with his or her needs or problems. (Or more simply) presenting reality to a person out of touch with it in a receivable way."

Even the intervention process is a starting point. Once the person admits a problem, you must be firm with consequences and keep the person on track toward finding outside help. Share options with your loved one and offer reasonable assistance. If the intervention does not work, you may need to try again or make some hard choices to take care of yourself. Ultimately, a person has to be ready for change. The intervention is designed to speed along that process.

Prochaska developed a model to illustrate the five stages of change:

1) pre-contemplation
2) contemplation
3) investigation/preparation
4) implementation
5) maintenance

Where does a loved one fall in this model? How about you?

You need supportive people at an intervention who have observed firsthand any of the stealing behaviors, the circumstantial clues of the behavior, or any other problems associated with the suspected or known behavior (mood swings, evasiveness, and change of lifestyle or interests). If you are the only one who can be involved in the intervention, so be it, but I would suggest you invite at least one trusted mutual friend, minister, counselor or family member to sit in.

An intervention is not a debate, discussion, or argument. You ask the person to listen as you and others outline and express your concerns (often in writing and read out loud) based on what you've observed as well as a sincere request for the person to get help immediately. Some resources are already researched and available should the person be ready to accept them. Sometimes the person will sit and listen without interruption, sometimes they will walk out, and sometimes they will interrupt throughout.

Here is an example of clues which might prompt an awareness that a loved one is stealing from work and how an attempt at an intervention may go:

You've noticed your spouse has been increasingly evasive or moody, agitated, even manic. Your spouse seems more emotionally guarded or distant. You've noticed over time an increase in your spouse's gift giving and in the higher quality of the gifts. Your spouse seems to spend money more freely.

Further, your spouse has stopped complaining about work–or begins complaining a lot more–and hasn't encouraged you to stop by the office for lunch lately.

Perhaps there's been a significant event in your spouse's life and/or your own–job-related or otherwise.

You may or may not have the benefit of knowing your spouse has previously had a problem with employee theft. But something seems fishy. You have asked your spouse if everything is okay and have brought up the specific mood changes and behaviors that concern you. Likely, your spouse has downplayed this.

You decide to talk to friends, family, and someone at your spouse's work–to get a reality check–to see if others have noticed changes in your spouse's mood or behavior. You find out from a co-worker that, indeed, your spouse has been acting differently at work, too–more agitated and, also, more obsessed with getting things perfect but, also, more disorganized. "Hmmm…" you think.

You suspect your spouse may have a problem with embezzling from work. You may not have the "smoking gun" which proves your spouse is stealing but you don't want to wait for that. There's too much at stake–getting fired, getting prosecuted, further loss of trust, and a delay in receiving help. Even if the intervention doesn't work–if your loved one denies a problem–it puts the person on notice you are not totally in the dark. He or she may seek or ask for help later more voluntarily.

"Dan" has arranged a time at home to get his wife "Lori's" undivided attention. He invited his wife's sister, "Susan," over because she's also suspected her of stealing from work.

Dan: "Honey, I'm glad you're here. Susan and I have something important to talk to you about and all we ask is that you listen. We'll give you a chance to talk when we're done. We need you to listen because we care about you."

Lori: "What's this about?"

Dan: "We're here because we care about you. We're here to talk about your work. We're not accusing you but we believe you are stealing from your job and we have reasons to believe this. We need you to listen to what we need to say."

Lori: "Stealing from my job? What are you talking about?"

Dan: "We know you feel shocked. But we need you to listen to our concerns. For the last two years we've noticed something different about you. You've been more agitated, more distant. We just need you to listen."

Lori: "What does this have to do with anything?"

Dan: "Let me finish. You've been spending more money on things–nice things–more gifts, more stuff. No offense, but that's not like you. Neither one of us has gotten a raise in a while. I've also noticed over the last two years since Erin went away to college that you quit going to the gym. I know we've been on a tighter budget since then but you haven't reduced your lifestyle at all. I'm not criticizing, I'm concerned. I went over our credit card bills the other day and it doesn't look like you've used those much. So I don't know where you're getting the money to spend like you do."

Lori: "What are you snooping around for? I have my own money you know! I don't need to account for everything I buy or bring into our house!"

Dan: "Please just listen to me: "I don't know how you are able to afford the gifts, the meals, and this increase in spending.""

Lori: "I don't keep track of things like I used to! You used to

183

complain that I was too tight with money–now I'm too loose with it? Make up your mind! I can't seem to do anything right! Not here, not at work! Nowhere! I buy people gifts and they complain! No wonder I'm spending money!"

Dan: "Honey, calm down. I'm just asking you to listen to our concerns. We care about you and know something is wrong."

Lori: "Nothing's wrong except for you accusing me. And what does this have to do with you, Susan?"

Susan: "Lori, I care about you and I know there's something wrong. Something's going on with you. I'm not sure if it's stealing or what. I know you used to shoplift and give stolen gifts to people–it seems like the same thing is happening again. If it's not shoplifting, I have a feeling you're doing something at work. I know you have access to money there. You've told me yourself how easy it would be for someone to take it without getting caught. Please just tell us. We want to help. We did some research and found out a lot of people steal from work when they have stress or other issues. You've been through a lot lately with Erin going to college and some of the things you told me a while ago that were happening at work."

Lori: "You always were the know-it-all, weren't you? Why are you meddling in this anyway?"

Susan: "Lori, we want to help you. You need to trust us. This secret you've been keeping has got to be eating you up inside. We promise. We just want to see you get some help. I miss the old Lori. We're not going to tell anybody else what's going on if that's what you're worried about. But we need you to tell the truth here and agree to get some help or there will be consequences."

Lori: "Consequences? Like what?"

Dan: "There have already been consequences: a loss of trust.

Lori, if you don't get honest here, I don't think our marriage can survive. I don't think you can survive. If you don't get help, I will. I'll go to a counselor myself and find out what I need to do. In the meantime, if you are stealing from work, eventually you're going to get caught, fired, and prosecuted. If you don't take this opportunity for help now, I won't be the one to bail you out."

Lori: "You don't have to worry about me."

Dan: "This is a sickness. I need you to tell me the truth."

Susan: "Lori, I need to be able to trust you, too. I need to feel comfortable about having you over our house. I don't need any fancy gifts and neither do my kids. We want to have the real Lori back."

Lori: "I've never stolen anything from your house! "All I've ever done is give to all of you. I've given my life for you. Nobody appreciates what I've had to sacrifice."

It is best to let the person vent for a bit if they need to.

Lori: (on the verge of tears) "There's just so much pressure. I don't know how to handle it. I'm always last. I don't ask for anything. I have needs, too. Nobody seems to notice."

Dan: (resisting the urge to save her) "It's okay, honey. That's why we're here. We can work on things together but only if I know what's really wrong. But first, we need to know: Have you been stealing from work?"

Lori: (after a long pause and a deep inhale) "Yes."

Dan: "And are you willing to stop and get help today?"

Lori: "What kind of help? You're not going to tell my boss, are you? I can't take any time off work."

Susan: "Lori, we're not going to tell anybody anything right now. That should be up to you and a therapist. But you need to get help right now before things get worse. You can take a medical leave if need be, whatever, just do it. Do it for you. We have the name of a therapist who specializes in theft issues."

Lori: "Don't tell Erin. I feel so ashamed. I don't know how this happened to me. I don't know how I got into this mess!"

Dan: "I don't know either but somebody's gonna help you figure it out so you can get help. You're gonna get through this. You're gonna make this right. We'll stand by you if you take that step."

Lori: "I guess I don't have a choice. I guess I have to."

Dan: "No, you have a choice… and so do we. And we're not going to choose to just watch you ruin your life and ours. We can't be a part of that. That's our choice."

Lori: "Okay. I hear you. I'm so afraid. I know I need help. I need your support."

Dan and Susan: "You've got it."

Notes & Reflections:

The Family Needs Help, Too

Just as a recovering alcoholic's family needs to be educated about the disease of alcoholism, so do the loved ones of the person who has been stealing from work. Just as the family of an alcoholic may attend Alanon or need therapy, the same is true for those affected by the person who has stolen.

Addiction is a family issue. Employee theft is a family issue. Success for all family members rests on healthy family members who know how to take care of themselves and offer the most appropriate means of support to others.

What does it feel like to be going through this?

_____

_____

_____

_____

_____

_____

What is your strategy to take care of yourself and also to support your loved one in a healthy, positive way? List some ideas and action steps.

1.   6.

2.   7.

3.   8.

4.   9.

5.   10.

Starting a Self-Help Group

Here are some ideas I've used to start & maintain C.A.S.A.:

1. Establish a meeting place and time

2. Create flyers and mail, post and fax about town especially to courts, churches, counseling offices, newspapers, criminal defense attorneys, bookstores, coffee shops (include a contact phone number or e-mail)

3. Contact the media (TV, radio, newspapers, magazines)

4. Create a website

5. Post flyers at other support group meetings

6. List your group information with your state's self-help clearinghouse–usually located in your state's capital

7. Write an article (even anonymously) for a paper

8. Notify employers/businesses or employee assistance and human resources departments that may pass on the word

9. Ask for ideas or help from friends/family

10. List in your local newspaper's health calendar

List some of your ideas:

1.   6.

2.   7.

3.   8.

4.   9.

5.   10.

__Epilogue__

Where do we go from here?

In the thirteen years since I started C.A.S.A. and embarked upon this personal and professional journey, I have grown in knowledge, compassion, and strength. I have been blessed to have created and been given numerous opportunities to share my story of struggle and success. At times it has been a lonely journey; at others, exhilarating.

I have done what I can to reach out to others and help them in various ways, to bring awareness to the public at large about employee theft. Writing this book is yet another way of getting the word out to more people, to push this issue "over the hump."

I know I will always need help. I pray there are others ready to start groups. I pray there are other professionals seeking education on how to best treat addictive-compulsive theft. I pray people in general open their minds and their hearts to those who suffer from these afflictions. I hope this book proves recovery is possible and paves a way there.

I see more and more businesses and companies embracing new ways of looking at employee theft–adopting better deterrence and prevention strategies as well as more treatment and rehabilitative options.

I truly believe each person who gets help not to steal makes a ripple wave of hope in the pool of solutions and, ultimately, helps make a better world.

As I continue my recovery, I don't know what's next in the design plan for me or for this "movement." I do know I am here to enjoy life.

Resources

*Terrence Shulman, Therapist, Attorney & Consultant
PO Box 250008 Franklin, MI 48025
Phone/Fax 248-358-8508
E-mail: info@shopliftersanonymous.com
Web sites: www.terrenceshulman.com
                www.theshulmancenter.com
                www.employeetheftsolutions.com
                www.shopliftersanonymous.com
                www.shopaholicsanonymous.org

*Cleptomaniacs And Shoplifters Anonymous, Detroit, MI
PO Box 250008 Franklin, MI 48025
(248) 358-8508

*Shoplifters Anonymous Manhattan, NY
Attention: Leo R. e-mail: sa515@earthlink.net
(212) 673-0392
http://home.earthlink.net/~sa514/index/html

*Shoplifters Anonymous Minneapolis, MN
Attention: Lois L. e-mail: lois@webblake.net
(763) 784-1535

*Cleptomaniacs And Shoplifters Anonymous, Philadelphia
Attn: Alyssa
Meets Mondays 6:30-7:30pm at Plymouth Meeting Church
on the Mall Room #8

*Cleptomaniacs And Shoplifters Anonymous, Los Angeles
Attn: Susan
Meets Mondays 6-7:30 at 5521 Grosvenor Blvd.,
Los Angeles, CA

*Shoplifters Recovery Program San Francisco, CA
Web site: www.shopliftersrecoveryprogram.com
Attention: Elizabeth Corsale, MA
1738 Union Street, Ste. 300
San Francisco, CA 94123
Phone: 415-267-6916

*Dr. Jon Grant, MD
Department of Psychiatry
University of Minnesota Medical Center.
2450 Riverside Avenue
Minneapolis, MN 55454
612-273-9800

*Margo Bristow, MSW
1142 W. Chicago Ave. Ste. 2 West
Oak Park, IL, 60302
(847) 791-1651

*Cynthia Marcolina, MA, LPC
203 Broad St.
Souderton, PA 18964
(215) 256-6265

*Betty Russell-Smayda
e-mail: russellsmayda@look.ca
British Columbia, Canada

Books

*Terrence Daryl Shulman, Something for Nothing: Shoplifting Addiction and Recovery, 2004

*John E. Grant, JD, MD and S.W. Kim, MD, Authors of Stop Me Because I Can't Stop Myself: *Taking Control of Impulsive Behavior*, 2002

*Marcus Goldman, MD Boston, MA, Author of Kleptomania, 1997

*John Case, Employee Theft: The Profit Killer, 2000

*Frank Abagnale, Catch Me If You Can, 1980

*Sgt. James Nelson and Ofc. Terry Davis, Protect Your Business, 1994

*Burt Rapp, Shoplifting and Employee Theft Investigation, 1989

*Snyder, Broome, Kehoe, McIntyre and Blair, Reducing Employee Theft, 1991

*Julie Williams, Pyromania, Kleptomania and Other Impulse Control Disorders, 2002

Vernon Johnson, Intervention, 1986